Seashells of North Carolina

Seashells of North Carolina

Revised & Expanded Edition

Edited by
Katie Mosher
with Arthur Bogan,
Edgar Shuller,
Douglas Wolfe,
and Erika Young

The University of North Carolina Press
CHAPEL HILL

A SOUTHERN GATEWAYS GUIDE

Designed by Lindsay Starr
Set in Warnock Pro and Helvetica Now Text
by Rebecca Evans

Cover photographs courtesy John Timmerman,
Edgar Shuller, and Scott Taylor.

Library of Congress Cataloging-in-Publication Data
Names: Mosher, Katie, editor. | North Carolina Sea Grant College
    Program, author.
Title: Seashells of North Carolina / North Carolina Sea Grant ;
    edited by Katie Mosher.
Other titles: Southern gateways guide.
Description: Revised and expanded edition. | Chapel Hill : The University
    of North Carolina Press, 2024. | Series: A Southern gateways guide |
    Includes bibliographical references and index.
Identifiers: LCCN 2024008371 | ISBN 9781469678948 (paperback ;
    alk. paper) | ISBN 9781469678955 (epub) | ISBN 9798890887573 (pdf)
Subjects: LCSH: Shells—North Carolina—Handbooks, manuals, etc. |
    Mollusks—North Carolina—Handbooks, manuals, etc. | BISAC:
    NATURE / Animals / Marine Life | NATURE / Regional
Classification: LCC QL415.N8 S4 2024 | DDC 594.09756—dc23/eng/20240312
LC record available at https://lccn.loc.gov/2024008371

Contents

A section of color plates follows page 78.

Foreword

....

SEASHELLS ARE ICONS of our North Carolina coast, offering inspiration for art and science. They provide the history of family vacations and ancient communities as well as ecosystems past and present. Thus, with great pride and many thanks, North Carolina Sea Grant offers this updated edition of *Seashells of North Carolina*.

After initial discussions with the University of North Carolina Press about an update, I contacted Arthur Bogan, curator of mollusks for the North Carolina Museum of Natural Sciences, in the North Carolina Department of Natural and Cultural Resources. Art offered to host a meeting and suggested we include the North Carolina Shell Club as another key partner. Not only did that session get us on our way, but I had a personal tour of the museum's extensive shell collection.

The challenge ahead was daunting, to say the least.

The previous edition of this book, with its multiple reprintings, has been revered by beachcombers and researchers alike. It served educators and learners at all levels and locations: classrooms and clubs, aquariums and universities, and laboratories and surf zones. Our goal has been to continue to serve all those audiences.

"*Seashells of North Carolina* has been a valuable resource to the North Carolina environmental education community," Lisa Tolley, environmental education program manager at the North Carolina Office of Environmental Education and Public Affairs, noted in a story in NC Sea Grant's *Coastwatch* magazine, written by Danielle Costantini, to honor the twentieth anniversary of the book. "The beauty and diversity of seashells found in North Carolina provide many 'teachable moments' for both children and adults."

That article highlighted Hugh Porter, the guide's original author, as Mr. Seashell. The NC Shell Club, of which Hugh and his wife Pinky were founding members, couldn't have agreed more with this distinction.

"In May 1989, Hugh and Pinky Porter were elected to honorary life membership in the NC Shell Club," notes Douglas Wolfe in a biography of Hugh he developed for the shell club's website. In 1996, the club began awarding the Hugh Porter Award at its annual shell show to recognize the exhibit that best features the mollusks of the western Atlantic, including the Boreal, Virginian, Carolinian, and/or Caribbean provinces.

Doug, who retired from the National Oceanic and Atmospheric Administration, including many years at the Beaufort Laboratory, was among our NC Shell Club experts. He provided critical reviews and drafts for updates to introductory sections. Our team also included Edgar Shuller, who represented the club at that first meeting and who is active in the Conchologists of America. Ed was key to updating the organization and confirming current scientific names for the shell descriptions. He also reviewed specimens from the Porter collection remaining at the University of North Carolina at Chapel Hill's Institute of Marine Sciences for updated images. Mark Johnson also provided identifications and other valuable input.

Art Bogan also continued his multiple roles in providing reviews and details across all sections of the book, providing access to the NC Museum of Natural Sciences' full collection, and updating photos. We anticipate that Art, as well as Jamie M. Smith, the collection manager in the museum's mollusk section, will continue as partners for outreach regarding mollusks and their amazing shells.

On our NC Sea Grant team, I relied on Erika Young, our education specialist and former faculty member at the University of North Carolina Pembroke, for her science as well as insight as to how the guide could be used. Nan Pincus Zarkar, an editor on our communications team, drew upon her education experience with youth and adults, as well as her copy editing skills. Carrie Clower, currently a doctoral student at North Carolina State University, was a key proofreader in our final push. Also Susan White, our director, has supported our focus on this product.

If you had used—and loved—the earlier edition, you will find this edition includes new illustrations from Georgia Minnich, whose career has included many years as exhibits curator at the North Carolina Aquarium at Pine Knoll Shores. She has provided new overall diagrams for bivalves and gastropods as well as an extensive guide to shell shapes as the first steps for beachcombers seeking to identify their finds.

A substantial change for the book has been an extensive rearrangement of shell descriptions to help guide identification. We also added some species and removed others that are not commonly found. Our team organized the species

to reflect more accurately the latest thinking in nomenclature and classification. In fact, this edition contains many changes in genus names, some new
family names, and a few entirely new names of species. Those changes reflect
advancements in science that the team explains in more detail in the preface
and throughout the book.

Also, I personally appreciate the guidance of Lucas Church at UNC Press,
and his colleagues Thomas Bedenbaugh, Mary Caviness, and Madge Duffey.
Brian Eller of NC State University's Office of Research Commercialization
ensured key steps for securing the copyright requirements for publication.

Please explore and enjoy not only this updated guide but also the lifetime of
discovery as you encounter new and familiar seashells on our North Carolina
coast.

Katie Mosher
Communications Director,
North Carolina Sea Grant

Preface

THIS SEASHELLS FIELD GUIDE has a long history. It started as a 32-page pamphlet (Porter and Tyler, 1971) published by the North Carolina Department of Natural and Economic Resources, which was reprinted with only a minor revision in 1981 by North Carolina Sea Grant. In the mid-1990s, lead author Hugh J. Porter worked with the Sea Grant team on a significant update, where it became much more than a pamphlet. With 132 pages, 82 additional species, updated common and scientific names, a new title, and new photography, it became popular among shell collectors and environmental educators, with distribution including by the University of North Carolina Press.

Reading *Seashells of North Carolina* has encouraged beachcombers of all ages. In recent years, this new edition was developed by NC Sea Grant, based at North Carolina State University, with partners from the North Carolina Shell Club and the North Carolina Museum of Natural Sciences, within the North Carolina Department of Natural and Cultural Resources.

Honoring Hugh J. Porter

Born in Ohio in 1928, Hugh Porter earned his degree in Pennsylvania, served in the US Army during the Korean conflict, then went on to earn his master's degree from the University of Delaware, becoming one of its first marine science graduates. But it is here in North Carolina that he made his career, joining the staff of the University of North Carolina at Chapel Hill's Institute of Marine Sciences in Morehead City in 1955 as an assistant in mollusk research, then progressing in faculty ranks and as a revered malacologist, with over forty scholarly articles, two marine atlases, and books to his credit. He also was a community leader, from taking on roles at his church to playing trombone in a dance band.

Hugh initiated the Institute of Marine Sciences' collection of marine mollusks in 1956 and served as curator of that collection throughout his long career. Under his care and direction, the institute's mollusk collection grew to about 25,000 lots before its transfer in two stages (1996 and 2012) to the NC Museum of Natural Sciences in Raleigh, where it now resides. Although Hugh officially retired from the faculty at the institute in 1996, he continued to come into his office in a part-time emeritus status for decades.

He was a founding and charter member of the NC Shell Club in 1957 and served the club in several capacities, including multiple terms as president. In September 1966, Governor Dan K. Moore recognized Hugh with membership in the Order of the Long Leaf Pine, one of North Carolina's highest honors. The award honored Hugh's central role in attracting the annual conference of the American Malacological Union to the state—and his role in making North Carolina the first state to have a state shell, with the selection and advocacy of the Scotch Bonnet.

Hugh organized the early shell shows sponsored by the club, and as a result of his leadership, these shows have become annual events that draw exhibitors, collectors, and visitors from distant states. Hugh passed away in December 2014, but his legacy lives on, including in the annual North Carolina Shell Show.

Scientific Updates

This new edition is the result of Hugh's vision, along with NC Sea Grant's understanding of how advances in science impact every field. In particular it considers updates in taxonomic classification—the study of the evolutionary history and relationships among or within groups of organisms. The classifications provide a phylogenetic tree, a diagram containing a hypothesis of the relationships that reflect the evolutionary history of a group of organisms.

For many years, species of mollusks were determined first by study of their physical characteristics and later the study of the soft parts. Now, DNA analysis provides a new tool to better understand relationships among mollusks. As a result of these advances, many scientific names have been revised in recent years.

Because they are never static, the taxonomy and names are subject to additional changes. The identifications in this guide reflect the naming provided in MolluscaBase (www.molluscabase.org) as of late 2022, with additional updates through late 2023. The scientific updates are an indication of the continuous nature of learning as we try to understand life on this planet.

You also will notice that we have added more than a dozen new species in the descriptions and removed a few that are not currently commonly found on North Carolina's coastal shores or in its waters.

Acknowledgments

THIS NEW EDITION builds upon North Carolina Sea Grant's 1997 publication of *Seashells of North Carolina*, written by Hugh Porter and Lynn Houser and edited by Jeannie Faris Norris, with photography by Scott Taylor.

The updates include contributions made by many individuals, including Arthur Bogan, PhD, and Jamie M. Smith of the North Carolina Museum of Natural Sciences; Douglas Wolfe, PhD, and Edgar Shuller Jr. of the North Carolina Shell Club; and Erika Young, PhD, Anna P. Zarkar, Carrie Clower, and Katie Mosher from NC Sea Grant. Illustrations for the new edition are by Georgia Minnich. In addition to Scott Taylor's photos, images for this edition were added from Arthur Bogan, John Timmerman, Douglas Wolfe, Edgar Shuller, and Anne Fogleman, Dora Zimmerman, and Mark Johnson. Cover art includes the work of Scott Taylor, John Timmerman, and Edgar Shuller.

The museum, within the North Carolina Department of Natural and Cultural Resources, and the University of North Carolina at Chapel Hill's Institute of Marine Sciences provided access to their respective shell collections, including many collected by Hugh Porter in his role at the Institute of Marine Sciences. Some specimens shown in the book came from UNC–Chapel Hill research vessels, as well as from the state of North Carolina's environmental agencies, Duke University Marine Laboratory, and commercial fishing catches. Some specimens were from Hugh Porter's personal collection and a few were from the collection of Mark Johnson, who retrieved them from scuba dives off North Carolina's coast near Wilmington.

This updated edition, published by the University of North Carolina Press, has been supported by Grants NA18OAR4170069 and NA22OAR4170109 given by the National Oceanic and Atmospheric Administration's National Sea Grant College Program to NC Sea Grant, based at North Carolina State University.

Seashells of North Carolina

Meet the Mollusks

FOR MANY PEOPLE, seashells are just part of the scenery on a beach. But other folks follow the tides that continually wash ashore and expose shells, many of them broken, worn, and eroded but still with interesting and unusual patterns, shapes, textures, and colors. The sea provides a natural treasure hunt, as many beachgoers make shell selections based on size, shape, color, or smoothness to later craft them into household decorations and jewelry.

Other collectors are fascinated by the science of the creatures that produce these shells. They enjoy looking at a shell to gain a deeper understanding of how these animals evolved and how they contribute to the coastal ecosystem. At any time, a group of shells lying inconspicuously in the sand may contain a rarity, just waiting to catch the shell enthusiast's eye.

Many people want to learn more when their curiosity is piqued on the beach. Perhaps they discover an intriguing shape poking out from the sand after a storm and search for it in a guide like this one. Others might, by chance, meet an experienced sheller on the beach. Talking with a collector passionate about shells is likely to spark interest in anyone who has at least a passing curiosity.

A walk down the beach is never the same once you begin to recognize some of the shells. Gradually you learn to use certain marks that aid in shell identification. The walk becomes more satisfying as you begin to recognize familiar shells as old friends, and it becomes more exciting as you search out and discover new ones.

Collectors and shell enthusiasts learn much more than the names of the shells. They not only become familiar with the animals that produce and occupy the shells but also learn where and when certain finds are most likely. They learn about tides, currents, and physical features of the coast. They discover that many shell identification marks relate to the animal's anatomy, habitat, and behavior.

Before long, collectors and shell enthusiasts have learned biology, physics, and geography without even realizing it. Such incidental knowledge encourages people to observe their environment more closely and to gain a better understanding of it. As a result, they may become better teachers and more conscientious stewards of our coastal environment. To that end, this guide was initially produced and recently updated to lead you on a journey of discovery, knowledge, and appreciation.

Geography Matters

More than 1,000 kinds of mollusks have been reported to live in North Carolina's estuaries and coastal and offshore marine waters, and most of them produce a shell as they grow. Upon full maturity, mollusks' shells range in size from quite small—less than 1 mm, or ⅕ of an inch—to over 450 mm, or nearly 18 inches, long.

This book is intended to assist in identification of the mollusk shells most likely to be encountered and collected on North Carolina's beaches and shallow coastal waters.

North Carolina is uniquely located at the juncture of major oceanographic currents of the North Atlantic Ocean. This circulation is dominated by the Gulf Stream, which brings tropical Caribbean waters around the tip of Florida and then north along the southeastern continental shelf edge close to Cape Hatteras. There, the Gulf Stream meets the southerly flow of the much cooler Labrador Current that brings Arctic waters all the way from Greenland, around Cape Cod, and down across the extent of the continental shelf off the mid-Atlantic states. During colder winters, the flow of the Labrador Current strengthens and may sweep around Cape Hatteras—in the process pushing the Gulf Stream much farther offshore.

Thus, North Carolina's extremely dynamic system supports several very diverse and overlapping assemblages of mollusks, including:

North Carolina, with its many barrier
islands, sits strategically near the
Gulf Stream and Labrador Current.

Illustration by Georgia Minnich.
Courtesy of North Carolina Sea Grant.

Boreal (or Virginian) species, which occur north of Cape Cod or Newfoundland and range over the continental shelf and high-salinity bays southward to Cape Hatteras.

Trans-Hatteran species, which range generally between Cape Cod, Massachusetts, and Cape Canaveral, Florida.

Carolinian species, which occur on the inner continental shelf and in high-salinity bays south of Cape Hatteras and across the northern Gulf of Mexico to Texas and the Yucatán Peninsula of Mexico.

Caribbean species, which are generally restricted to the outer continental shelf and shelf edge, including many that range south as far as Brazil.

Estuarine species, which are restricted to low-salinity inshore waters along the Atlantic coast of North America.

Biology Basics

Mollusks are soft-bodied animals, and nearly all mollusks produce a shell that serves to provide structural support and protection for their soft parts. They create their shells from their mantle, concentrating minerals, mainly calcium, that they have absorbed or consumed from their environment. As the mollusk grows within its shell, the mantle generates and secretes a very specialized mixture of proteins along with very high concentrations of calcium carbonate, the primary constituent of the ultimate mollusk shell.

The proteins, known collectively as conchiolin, form a delicate structural matrix over and around which the calcium carbonate crystallizes in successive layers to form the very dense and strong protective rocklike shell for many mollusks. Although growth slows with age, this process continues as long as the mollusk lives.

Every living species possesses a unique combination of genetic materials, known as DNA, that is arranged in genes passed from parent to offspring. The genes determine and maintain the species characteristics. In recent years, scientists have learned that the protein mixture secreted by the molluscan mantle consists of hundreds of different molecular structures, many shared with other mollusks and others unique to the individual species. The remarkable range of variability and diversity among molluscan shell sizes, shapes, and color patterns is determined by the genetic materials, or the genome, carried within the individual species. Biological and evolutionary relationships are identified by similarity among the genomes of different species.

The geological record reveals mollusks already were a diverse group of organisms abundant in the world oceans 450 million to 500 million years ago. North Carolina's coastal plain is underlain by marine deposits containing a diverse assemblage of fossil mollusks from periods during the past 12 million to 15 million years, when the sea level was higher. The North Carolina Fossil Club has published useful illustrated guides to these shells, which can be collected in stream beds and with permission in commercial marl pits in several areas (Chandler and Timmerman, 2011; Timmerman and Chandler, 2008, 2020). There is even a fossil museum in Aurora.

Today's mollusks are highly diversified, living not only in the ocean but also in freshwater streams and lakes and on land. They are found from the tropics to polar regions and at elevations from sea level to tree line. This book is restricted to molluscan species that live in North Carolina's ocean or marine waters and in estuaries, where freshwater mixes with salt water through tidal action, including waters near the mouths of rivers and in our sounds.

North Carolina's shelled mollusks are classified into five classes: Bivalvia, Gastropoda, Polyplacophora, Scaphopoda, and Cephalopoda. The members of the classes Bivalvia and Gastropoda, better known as bivalves and gastropods, can be found in marine, brackish, and fresh waters. In contrast, the members of Polyplacophora, Scaphopoda, and Cephalopoda—also known as chitons, tuskshells, and squids and octopuses—are found only in marine environments.

With over 62,000 species, there are more different species of gastropods than any other class of mollusks. There are approximately 8,000 species of bivalves, 1,000 species of chitons, 820 species of squids and octopuses, and 600 species of tuskshells.

Mollusks are known for their shells. The few mollusks that do not produce a hard calcareous shell (including squids and octopuses, terrestrial slugs, and sea slugs) have evolved other protective strategies. These include color-changing or camouflage abilities; diversionary ink production, which creates a form of smoke screen; and reclusive cryptic behavior such as hiding during the day under leaves or rocks and coming out only at night. An additional protective strategy is the production of foul tastes and/or toxins, sometimes with associated bright colors. Some mollusks, such as the cone snails, may also use venom; some octopuses can also inject venom through the beak. Squids have an internal shell called a pen, made primarily of chitin and proteins. Cuttlefish have a calcareous cuttlebone. Beaks, pens, and cuttlebones are less common here.

Many mollusks produce a brownish "outer skin" called periostracum that covers some or all of the external surface of the shell and hides, or at least disguises, the colors and sculptures of the shell. When the animal dies, the periostracum usually erodes away, exposing the surface of the shell. The shells of many mollusks also serve as habitats or substrates for the growth of many other organisms—such as algae, bryozoans, tube-building worms, and corals—that also disguise the surface, color, and shape of the mollusk. Removing the traces of those fouling organisms can prove quite a challenge for the shell collector.

Bivalves

Bivalves are mollusks with two shells, or valves, right and left, which are connected by the ligament, an elastic and compressible structure at the top, or dorsal, part of the shells. The shells are connected on the inside by one or more powerful muscles that close the shells when contracted and allow the valves to open when relaxed. In most bivalves, the hinge is usually reinforced by closely fitting, interlocking hinge teeth in each valve. As the bivalve grows, it must continually not only extend the outer edge (and external sculpture) of the shell but also adjust the shape and proportions of the hinge area on the interiors of the paired shells as well—a truly remarkable achievement. Along with the shape and external sculpture of the shell, the precise location and shape of the ligament and the structural details of the hinge teeth are very important characteristics used in the identification of bivalves. (Learn more in "How to Use This Guide.")

Most bivalves have separate sexes, but a few are hermaphrodites (with both male and female sex organs), and some may switch, or alternate, sexes at different stages in their life history. Marine bivalves reproduce by releasing eggs and sperm directly into the surrounding water column, where random fertilization occurs and their complex two-stage larval development ensues. Bivalve eggs have limited yolk and hatch quickly into compact larvae, called trochophores, which in turn metamorphose into microscopic "swimming" larvae, called veligers, that become temporary members of the plankton community, feeding on smaller microalgae or phytoplankton as they develop their embryonic shells. The duration of these larval stages varies by species and with other factors such as water temperature. During this planktonic period, however, the larvae may be carried by ocean currents over great distances, and this dispersal strategy enables a species to colonize suitable habitats far from their point of origin.

BIVALVES

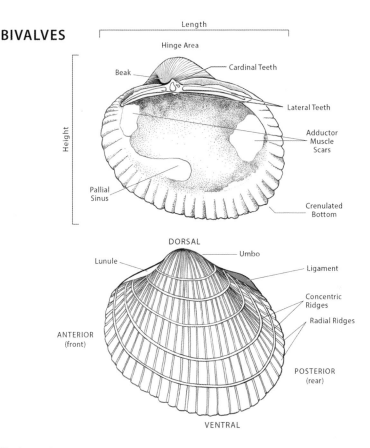

Bivalve anatomy.
Illustration by Georgia Minnich.
Courtesy of North Carolina Sea Grant.

Often within a few weeks, larvae complete development and settle out, now with a delicate miniature bivalve shell, onto their preferred substrate to grow into adults. Some bivalve species may complete their entire life cycle in a short time: growing to maturity, reproducing, and dying within one year. In North Carolina, the Bay Scallop reaches its maximum size and sexual maturity in two years, then reproduces and rarely survives a third season. Yet growth rings from a large Southern Quahog taken off Shackleford Banks suggest it lived 77 years or more. Other bivalves are known to live for over 100 years, such as Pacific Giant Clams and Ocean Quahogs, the latter up to 450 years.

Most bivalves are filter feeders. Water is drawn into their shell through one of two paired tubular extensions, or siphons, near the rear of the mantle and passed over the gills, which perform two essential functions. The gills extract oxygen from the incoming water and simultaneously release carbon dioxide. The gills also provide a filtering mechanism that separates tiny microscopic algae, known as phytoplankton, from the water and selectively moves that food toward the bivalve's mouth while discriminating against and discarding larger particles of suspended sediment and most zooplankton. The food is consumed, passed through the gut of the bivalve, and digested, and the feces are removed along with other waste by the continuing flow of water through the outflowing siphon. A few bivalves are deposit feeders. The tellins (in the family Tellinidae), for example, have long siphons that act like vacuum cleaners, sucking in algal cells from the surface of the sediments surrounding their burrows.

Various families of bivalves have adapted to life in particular habitats. Many groups have a strong muscular foot that enables them to burrow and move around in sand or soft sediment. Some bore deeply into sediments and move in their burrows. Others spin a set of strong fibers, called a byssus, by which they attach to rocks, shell fragments, marsh grass, or dock pilings. Still others cement their shells directly to rocks, other shells, or pilings and remain stationary throughout their lives. A few species bore into wood or soft rock and enlarge their burrows as they grow. Some scallops (Pectinidae) and fileclams (Limidae) live unattached and swim (however erratically) by clapping their two valves together and ejecting pulsating streams of water.

Gastropods

Gastropods are a very large and diverse group of mollusks also known as univalves or simply snails. A primary feature is a single, coiled shell that develops initially during the larval stage. In nudibranchs, or sea slugs, the shell does not continue to grow after the larval stage, and adults are essentially without shells. Terrestrial slugs have adapted to life in a calcium-deprived environment and generally produce no shell during their early development.

Sexes are separate in most marine gastropods, and some of the more primitive forms reproduce in much the same way as bivalves. For those, fertilization occurs externally in the water column, and larval development is two-phased, with trochophore and veliger larval stages. The veliger larvae generally start with bilateral symmetry but undergo torsion, or twisting, before the larval shell begins to grow.

In most gastropods, fertilization is internal, but then the females lay egg masses that take many different forms. For many gastropods, these egg masses look like formless blobs—but for the Florida Fighting Conch, they take the

GASTROPODS

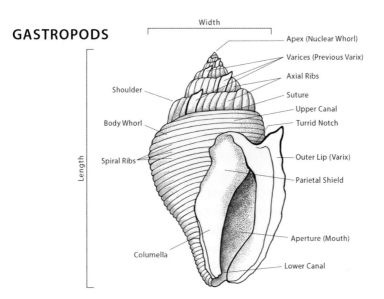

Gastropod anatomy.
Illustration by Georgia Minnich.
Courtesy of North Carolina Sea Grant.

form of gelatinous strands; for moonsnails, they take the form of sand collars. The state shell of North Carolina, the Scotch Bonnet, has egg masses that take the form of elaborate towerlike structures.

Compared to the eggs of bivalves, gastropods' eggs are relatively rich in yolk, and they develop further within the egg case and skip a planktonic trochophore stage to hatch directly into the planktonic veliger larval stage of development. Some gastropods, such as whelks and cones, lay yolk-rich eggs in encapsulated cases that protect and nourish the larvae throughout early development. The young hatch directly as miniature adults, often without any planktonic stage. Whelk egg cases often surprise beach visitors.

During the planktonic veliger stage for most gastropods, sometimes only a few days but generally two weeks to two months, larvae develop a delicate miniature spiral shell, which becomes the tip of the spire in the adult shell and is called the protoconch, or early shell. Gastropods that undergo their larval metamorphosis within the egg capsules (so-called direct development, without planktonic larvae) tend to have a smaller, shorter protoconch than those with planktonic stages. That can be useful in identifying the adult shell. Gastropods with indirect planktonic development produce many more eggs than those with direct development and, because of predation upon their larvae, have a much lower survival rate.

DISTINCTIVE WHORLS AND MORE

Each full turn of the gastropod shell is called a whorl, beginning at the protoconch and ending with the last and usually the largest, called the body whorl. The gastropod extends and retracts its body into the shell through the opening, or aperture, at the face of the body whorl. The edge of the gastropod mantle lies just inside the outer lip of the aperture, and shell growth occurs through the mantle's secretion of fresh conchiolin matrix and calcium carbonate along that growing edge of the shell, continually enlarging the body whorl and producing species-specific external shell sculpture and color patterns as it grows. Many gastropods maintain a thin outer lip during early fast-growing stages and merely thicken their outer lips as they approach maturity. For gastropods— including cowries, the Scotch Bonnet, and the Florida Fighting Conch—the shape of the adult shell may be radically different from that of the juvenile or immature forms.

Unlike bivalves, gastropods have a distinct head with paired tentacles. The tentacles are chemosensory organs, enabling the snail to detect and locate food or to avoid predators. Some gastropods also have eyes that can detect shadows and movements in their surroundings.

Gastropods also have a large muscular foot and glide across or through substrate or sediment on a series of wavelike contractions. Many gastropods have a hard leathery operculum, or "trapdoor," that tightly closes the aperture when the body is completely retracted. Gastropods take in oxygen from water, drawing the water into their mantle cavities and over their gills through a siphon, which is extended through an opening, or siphonal canal, located near the front of the body whorl and aperture. By probing in different directions with their siphon, they can locate and move toward prospective prey.

Most gastropods are carnivores that prey on other animals. A few primitive gastropods, such as abalones and limpets, are herbivores and graze on algae attached to the substrates on which they live. Many are scavengers or detritivores, feeding on dead animal and plant material. The gastropod's head contains a muscular tubelike extension called a proboscis, with a mouth at the forward end with a ribbonlike strip of teeth called a radula just inside. Herbivores use their radula to scrape algae away from other substrates. Carnivores use it to drill holes in the shells of other mollusks or tear the flesh of their prey, whatever it may be.

The spacing, arrangement, and shape of the radular teeth are different for each type of gastropod and are used by experts to assist in the identification and classification of gastropods. Most of the cones, terebras, and turrids possess a venom gland. Their radular teeth are shaped like tubular harpoons or darts, capable of immobilizing or killing their prey, usually small worms or other, smaller mollusks. A few large Indo-Pacific cones routinely kill and consume small fish, and there are documented instances of human deaths from their neurotoxic stings.

Polyplacophora

This group includes the chitons, limpet-like mollusks with eight articulated shelly plates, neatly enclosed in a leathery ring of tissue called the girdle. The entire class includes about 1,000 species (Rosenberg, 2014), mostly tropical in distribution. Reproduction is by external fertilization and indirect development, with trochophore and veliger larval stages, much like bivalves and primitive gastropods. Shell growth involves synchronized enlargement of all eight plates, which cover the back of the bilaterally symmetrical animal. Chitons generally adhere tightly to a "home spot" on hard substrates such as rocks, pilings, and other shells, and they are herbivores, using their radula to graze on attached algae in their immediate vicinity. North Carolina's most common species are small, and it is rare to find one washed ashore. It will most likely still be alive and attached to a larger shell.

Scaphopoda

These are the tuskshells, aptly named for their shape like an elephant's tusk. This is another small class, with about 600 species (Rosenberg, 2014) worldwide. Several species occur in North Carolina waters, but most live in deep water off the edge of the continental shelf and are unlikely to be encountered. Scaphopods draw seawater into and out of their mantle cavity through the small aperture at the top of the shell. The animals are carnivores that burrow into surface sediments and use specialized sticky feeding tentacles to capture their microscopic prey. Their reproduction is similar to that of bivalves, chitons, and primitive gastropods, with two-stage larval development. Shell growth occurs at the edge of the mantle, along the nearly circular rim of the body aperture at the large end of the shell. Two major families of scaphopods occur in North Carolina. Shells of the few common shallow-water species can be found in beach drift.

Cephalopoda

There are about 800 living species (Rosenberg, 2014) of cephalopods. These include the Chambered Nautilus, cuttlefish, squids, and octopuses, which are the most anatomically complex and behaviorally advanced mollusks. Another major group of cephalopods, the ammonites, was extremely diverse in world oceans before they became extinct at the end of the Cretaceous period, about 66 million years ago.

Cephalopods reproduce with internal fertilization and direct development; that is, the young hatch from the encapsulated eggs as miniature adults. Only a few cephalopod species produce a hard calcareous shell, with the best known being the Chambered Nautilus, with four species that occur only in the tropical Pacific Ocean. A very unique squid relative, however, is the Ram's Horn Squid, which lives in tropical waters worldwide, including the Gulf Stream off North Carolina's coast. The exquisite internal shells of the Ram's Horn Squid are sometimes found on beaches south of Cape Hatteras after storms.

Another specialized cephalopod group is the argonauts, related to octopuses. Female argonauts produce a calcareous egg case, called a paper nautilus, which they in turn occupy (without any physical anatomical attachment) and in which they carry and care for their once-in-a-lifetime batch of fertile eggs until they hatch. The argonauts swim in open water and are preyed upon by large fish. Their beautiful "shells" are occasionally found in fish stomachs, and very rarely, one may wash ashore on the beach.

Harvests and Impacts

Archaeological research has revealed much about the human use of mollusks and their shells. In North America, native coastal populations relied on shellfish for food and as containers and utensils. Shells were also used as ornaments and jewelry, and some were fashioned into beads and woven into strings or belts; these were known as wampum and valued as currency. Shells of the

Lightning Whelk (and implements made from them) found in burial mounds have demonstrated that these items were being conveyed nearly 1,000 years ago to Hopewell communities more than 500 miles inland.

The North Carolina Division of Marine Fisheries reports catch and value data for several categories of mollusks harvested commercially in the state: hard clams, oysters, various scallops, and whelks/conchs as a combined category. Annual commercial harvests of most of these species have fluctuated. One noticeable trend is that since 2000, commercial stocks have increased, reflecting a steady growth of shellfish aquaculture, especially for oysters.

In the mid-to-late 1800s, the Chesapeake Bay was a hub for oyster harvests, with large dredge boats working deep waters. Those harvests depleted not only the source of oyster spat, or larvae, that sustain the population but also its habitat. When the Chesapeake fishery was collapsing from overfishing in the early 1880s, dredge boats moved to North Carolina's sounds, where oysters were abundant. Local oyster canneries were quickly established or enlarged in Elizabeth City, New Bern, and other coastal towns. To protect local jobs, officials ordered that state waters be off-limits to out-of-state dredge boats.

In 1897, North Carolina oyster production peaked, with nearly 5.8 million pounds of oyster meat landed and processed. A year later it was down by 25 percent, and ten years later it was down by 66 percent from the peak. Fast-forward to the 2020s, and the state reports that average annual commercial production is growing once again, but the number of pounds of oyster meat landed and processed in-state is still less than 20 percent of its peak in 1897. Also, note that a bushel of oysters in the shell generally produces about 7 pounds of wet oyster meats (North Carolina Department of Environmental Quality, Division of Marine Fisheries, n.d.a; Tabb, 2018).

SHELLFISH AQUACULTURE

The North Carolina shellfish aquaculture industry shows potential for continued growth. Adults can be conditioned to spawn, and larvae can be grown to juvenile stages in hatcheries and nurseries. Sometimes free-swimming oyster larvae are moved to setting tanks containing a substrate, or cultch, such as oyster shells. Upon setting, larvae metamorphose to the sessile (static) adult form and permanently attach themselves to the substrate. These tiny juveniles are called spat. The substrate, containing clusters of spat, can then be moved.

In aquaculture, larvae set on individual grains of microcultch, or finely ground oyster shells. The spat quickly outgrow the microcultch and become oysterseed. These young, individual oysters, known as singles, are then stocked into mesh bags or cages that float in or on the water column or rest just off the bottom. Bags or cages are periodically flipped to help reduce biofouling. Cultured oysters with deep cups are highly desired by chefs.

Similarly, clam seed can be grown to juveniles in flow-through seawater tanks and then planted in natural environments for grow-out to market size. Cultured hard clams, or quahogs, of a uniform size are increasingly showing up in restaurants. With funding from North Carolina Sea Grant, researchers and growers are studying the potential of the beautiful and delicious Sunray Venus (*Macrocallista nimbosa*) as an aquaculture species.

WILD HARVESTS

Commercial harvests for shellfish have varied over the years. For example, the continental shelf off Cape Lookout and Onslow Bay has supported valuable beds of Atlantic Calico Scallops. Maintenance of that population has been largely dependent on an upstream source of planktonic larvae. During the 1960s and '70s, the commercial potential of these populations was discovered and quickly overexploited in North Carolina and Florida. Trawlers brought in deckloads of scallops, overwhelming local shucking facilities initially set up to process inshore Bay Scallops. Automated shucking equipment was quickly developed and installed, first at the shore-based locations and then on the trawlers themselves. The North Carolina Division of Marine Fisheries regulates the scallop fishery, taking trips offshore to evaluate whether the scallop population there could support a limited open season.

North Carolina's Bay Scallop fishery and harvest has had related problems. Prior to about 1930, these inshore scallops were not fished commercially. Harvests ensued with dredges that damaged the seagrass beds that are the preferred habitat for the scallops, with populations declining as a result. Restrictions on dredges brought temporary restoration of the harvest, but in many areas, seagrass still shows effects of pollution and disease.

The Sea Scallop occurs off North Carolina only on the deeper parts of the continental shelf north of Cape Hatteras. That population has supported harvests from 1978 to 2020, suggesting that the harvests under current regulatory and management practices may be sustainable.

Since about 1980, whelks have supported a very small but steady fishery harvest in the state. Annual harvests between 2010 and 2020 were up to four times the size of those during the previous 30 years. Given the history of unsustainable harvests of other commercial mollusk species, and the four-to-seven-year maturation period for whelk development, there are questions. Some whelks also are sequential hermaphrodites. Because females may reach maturity at a later age and larger size, they are more vulnerable to harvest than males.

When gathering mollusks of any species for personal consumption, you must follow state regulations, such as collecting only from state-approved shellfish waters. Some areas are posted as closed areas and identified as polluted, usually with fecal coliform bacteria from shoreline development and runoff. The state also will issue temporary closures after storms, with those notices posted online. Under limited conditions, blooms of planktonic red tide may also occur in coastal waters, rendering the local shellfish toxic to humans. Such blooms are usually detected before their arrival in the state. The North Carolina Department of Environmental Quality's Shellfish Sanitation and Recreational Water Quality webpage is frequently updated, serving as your best guide to knowing where you can safely harvest.

EXOTIC SPECIES

Another major human practice that results in significant ecological and economic damage to native mollusk populations is the careless or clueless release of exotic species, including mollusks. Many notable examples have involved freshwater species, such as Zebra Mussels (*Dreissena polymorpha*), Quagga Mussels (*Dreissena bugensis*), Asian Clams (*Corbicula fluminea*), and Rapa Whelks (*Rapana venosa*).

The arrival of exotic species raises the risk of introducing unknown disease pathogens, pests, and predators into native populations. One way invasive species arrive is in the ballast water of oceangoing ships, which may be released into the waters at our ports. While other states have allowed nonnative shellfish to be introduced for aquaculture or to enhance wild stocks, in the 2020s, North Carolina's shellfish management plans focus on habitat restoration, harvest-free nursery zones, restricted harvest, and promotion of aquaculture.

Invasive shellfish species have been identified in nearby states. The Asian Green Mussel (*Perna viridis*), native to India and Southeast Asia, was first observed in the Caribbean around 1990. Since then, it has been found along the coasts of Florida, Georgia, and South Carolina. Its northerly range expansion may be limited by wintertime water temperatures. Watch for these mussels on jetties and beached materials. Report any suspected invasive species to the North Carolina Marine Patrol or local officials.

Shipworms, a bivalve in the family Teredinidae, have historically caused extensive damage to wooden vessels and structures like docks and bulkheads. Use of pressure-treated lumber (e.g., chromated copper arsenate) in marine construction can introduce toxins and cause ecological changes in nearby marine communities. Similarly, antifouling paint used on boat bottoms (such as the now-banned tributyl tin) can contaminate marine communities in boat basins and harbors, including species consumed by humans.

These examples illustrate the interactions of mollusks with the growing human population and emphasize the need for greater awareness and care in the future. We are still identifying how climate change and the associated acidification of global seas are impacting coastal mollusk populations.

Collecting and Studying Shells

Although few mollusks live on sandy beaches, the shoreline is always a good place to search for empty shells that have washed ashore. The time of day you visit the beach matters. The best times often will be at or near low tide, perhaps an hour before to an hour after. Or go early to enjoy sunrise—and to see what came ashore overnight.

Watch the calendar for "spring tides" that occur on new and full moons all year despite the name. Late winter or early spring—after winter nor'easters and other storms and before the arrival of summer crowds—is an excellent time to collect. Also, consider when beaches are safely reopened after tropical storms or hurricanes, often in August and September. Even smaller storm tides may cast large shells ashore, leaving them high on the beach.

Interesting shells sometimes can be found attached to flotsam or burrowed into pieces of driftwood washed ashore on the beach. With a sharp eye, a great variety of smaller shells, such as olivellas, wentletraps, and tuskshells, can be retrieved from the drift lines of the most recent high tides. Shells frequently accumulate in small pockets created by eddies in incoming waves. In January 1995, Hugh Porter, author of this book's previous edition and responsible for many of the species' descriptions you'll be reading soon, scraped up a bucketful of shell hash from a low-tide area of Bogue Banks in Carteret County. It contained intact shells and fragments of 109 species.

PLANNING AHEAD: COLLECTION GEAR

Shell-gathering tools may be items found at home or borrowed from friends:

A kitchen colander or strainer can be used to sift small shells out of fine sand or mud.

A larger sieve can readily be constructed from a few boards and a piece of wire mesh or hardware cloth. To retain the very small specimens, place a sheet of window screening beneath your sieve.

Low-tide collecting can also be quite successful on the shores and in shallow waters around the intertidal sand and mud flats of the state's sounds, bays, and estuaries. Be careful to avoid the strong currents near inlets. Our estuaries contain many habitats, from sandy to muddy bottoms, seagrass flats to intertidal salt marshes, and hard surfaces, including old shell fragments, seawalls, jetties, and reef-like beds of oysters. Each of these habitats may harbor species not found in any other. For those with proper training and supervision, snorkeling or scuba diving may reveal species very rarely found on beaches.

It's worth noting that the science of classifying and understanding mollusks has been advanced by scientists studying the mollusks and empty shells provided by the commercial fishing community. A. F. Chestnut, an early director of the University of North Carolina at Chapel Hill's Institute of Marine Sciences, found the first known living specimen of the very rare Coronado Bonnet on the deck of a trawler that had been fishing off Wimble Shoals near Oregon Inlet.

Another unexpected place scientists have found shells and mollusks is within sea stars. Hugh Porter learned that predaceous sea stars could be a source of a wide variety of small mollusks (Porter, 1972; Wells, Wells, and Gray, 1961). Several sea stars, such as *Astropecten articulatus*, *Astropecten duplicatus*, and *Luidia clathrate*, found in North Carolina coastal waters are carnivores that include small (up to 10 mm, or ⅜ inch) mollusks in their diets.

RESPONSIBLE COLLECTING

Follow a few guiding principles:

Minimize habitat disruption: If you turn over rocks, return them to their original positions to preserve the natural communities. Be selective. Do not overcollect. Serious collectors keep records of where and when they find specimens and the condition when collected. Thus, carry a pen and notebook on serious collecting trips, such as in new locations.

Avoid taking live specimens: This will limit harm to local populations and disruptions to the food web. Instead, try observing the specimens' appearance, habitat and behavior. Naturalist Rachel Carson, author of *Silent Spring*, did this as she wrote books such as *The Edge of the Sea* and *The Sea around Us*. She used words to describe sea life she found in tidal pools, on rocks, and in estuaries. In fact, you can visit a North Carolina Coastal Reserve site named for Carson, who worked nearby in Beaufort. You may keep a journal and draw a sketch of the mollusk with your own description. Or take a photo, which will also be helpful to identify the shell if you didn't bring your field guide.

If you tire of the hobby: Pass along your collection to family or friends. Or contact a shell club or a nature study group.

Find a club: The North Carolina Shell Club, founded in 1957, meets quarterly at various locations in the state, with educational programs and opportunities to exchange shells and participate in field trips. The club provides scholarships for university students, and is associated with the Conchologists of America, which draws membership from all over the world. Learn more online at www.ncshellclub.com.

How to Use This Guide

BASED ON EVOLUTIONARY and genetic characteristics, members of each of the five classes of mollusks are in turn classified into family groupings, with names ending in *idae*. The shell descriptions in this new edition of our guide are presented in scientific classifications. But do not let that scare you from starting your own shell collection. Shapes still matter.

When you find a shell, follow these steps:

1. Identify it as a bivalve or gastropod or other class of mollusk.

2. Consider that particular shell's general shape.

3. Match the overall shape to one of the groups provided later in this chapter by reviewing the related illustrations.

4. Review the few listed characteristics to narrow your options to a particular family. Or maybe a common name will help you.

5. Turn to the referenced page number for the shell descriptions.

6. Check the descriptions to match photos and details, including scientific and common names, range, habitat, and other notes.

7. Make the identification: the name for your shell.

8. Share your success with friends and family!

Challenges in Identification

Varied challenges arise in the world of identification. Many species bear strong resemblances to others that may or may not be closely related. Thus, you are encouraged to check similar-appearing species before making a final identification. Remember, too, that this guide focuses on shells most likely to be encountered. It is quite possible that you may find a rare or very small species not included here. If you cannot find your shell, you might check out some of the references in the resources section, including the listing of online resources that are more regularly updated. Or take your find to a meeting of the North Carolina Shell Club.

The size listed for each species points to a second challenge with shell identification, which is that shells change appearance across their life span. Mollusks are living, growing creatures, and small juvenile shells do not always closely resemble the fully adult form. For purposes of distinguishing and identifying the species in this book, "small" generally means less than 1 inch. "Medium" is 1 to 2 inches. "Large" generally indicates more than 2½ inches. In nearly all species descriptions, the measurement provided is for the length. In some cases, the width is more important, and thus that measurement is provided.

A third challenge relates to the color of shells. For each species, the variability of shell color and pattern is discussed in the species description, but it is important to remember that long-dead shells may have been sun-bleached on the beach or may have become stained by the long processes they experienced before you found your specimen. Shells often have been buried decades or sometimes even centuries before they are uncovered and washed ashore by dynamic wave action, currents, and beach erosion.

Black or gray shells likely have been buried for a long time with limited oxygen, such as in anoxic marsh sediments. Those shells also may have absorbed mineral sulfides. Specimens buried in the vicinity of wrecks containing iron parts may be stained reddish brown or yellow with iron oxides. Collectors should also note the colors of shells once they are in your collection, as colors may continue to fade over time if exposed to sunlight or even bright lights indoors.

Using the Detailed Shell Descriptions

For each shell, two names are given: the currently accepted scientific name and an official common name.

The scientific name consists of four parts: genus and species (both italicized) and author and date (not italicized). When a new shell is discovered, it is generally assigned to an existing genus (a group of very closely related species) and given a new unique species name, followed by the name of the author who described the species and a publication date for that species name.

Recognized scientific names are revised as scientists discover more about the evolutionary and genetic relationships among the mollusks in question—and as they realize other updates are needed to clarify names. If a particular species is shifted into a genus or family different from its original assignment, the author and date for that earlier species name is placed in parentheses. Scientific names presented here are those accepted by MolluscaBase (www .molluscabase.com) in spring 2022, with additional updates through late 2023.

Knowing previous names will be particularly helpful if you find it necessary to consult older references in your identification efforts.

The official common name is the one recommended by Turgeon et al. (1998) and updated if needed by MolluscaBase. For some species, alternate common names, particularly those used in North Carolina or elsewhere, are also provided.

The information on habitats describes where the mollusk is known to live in our state and suggests where you may find specimens washed ashore. Be aware that currents often carry shells to new locations. For example, you may find that oyster shells have traveled from estuarine waters through one of our many inlets and then are found on the ocean side of one of our barrier islands.

Shell descriptions may include terms that are new to you, but they identify common characteristics. If needed, check those terms in the glossary. Also review the general anatomy illustrations of bivalves and gastropods, provided on the inside back cover for easy reference.

Boldface species names within species descriptions indicate they have entries of their own.

Shell Shapes

As noted above, once you have determined that your shell is either a bivalve or a gastropod, you then want to determine its family name. For some species, this can be a daunting task because of overlapping species characteristics among families. Thus, this book will provide helpful hints.

Shapes and a few characteristics, presented below, are included where applicable in the family and species accounts in the next sections of the book.

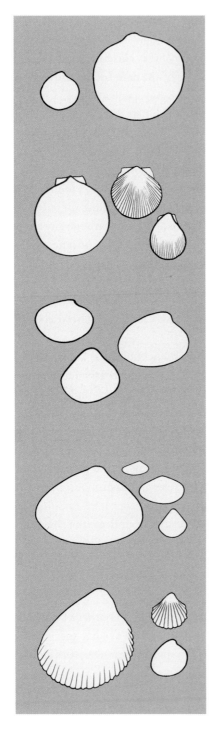

CIRCULAR
Glycymerididae: bittersweet clams
(pp. 45–46)
Lucinidae: lucine clams (pp. 62–65)
Veneridae (in part): venus clams (pp. 96–104)
Arcticidae (in part): Ocean Quahog (p. 68)
Ungulinidae: diplodon clams (p. 95)

CIRCULAR/OVAL WITH EARS
Pectinidae: scallops (pp. 56–59)
Limidae: fileclams (pp. 61–62)
Spondylidae: thorny oysters (pp. 59–60)

OVATE/EGG-SHAPED
Veneridae (in part): venus clams (pp. 96–104)
Cyrenoididae: marshclams (p. 76)
Arcticidae (in part): Ocean Quahog (p. 68)
Semelidae: semele clams (pp. 90–93)
Myidae (in part): softshell clams (pp. 104–5)
Lyonsiidae: lyonsia clams (p. 115)
Periplomatidae: spoonclams (p. 116)

TRIANGULAR
Mactridae: surfclams (pp. 76–80)
Donacidae: coquinas, wedge clams
(pp. 89–90)
Tellinidae: tellin clams (pp. 81–89)
Crassatellidae: crassatella clams
(pp. 66–67)
Corbulidae (in part): corbula clams
(pp. 105–7)

HEART-SHAPED
Cardiidae: cockles (pp. 68–72)
Carditidae: cardita clams (pp. 65–66)
Nuculidae: nutclams (p. 32)

Bivalve shapes guide.
Illustration by Georgia Minnich.
Courtesy of North Carolina Sea Grant.

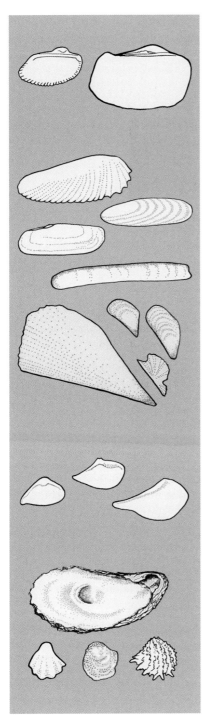

RECTANGULAR
With nearly straight hinge line.
  Arcidae: ark shells (pp. 40–44)
  Noetiidae: false ark clams (pp. 46–47)
  Hiatellidae: hiatella clams, geoducks
    (pp. 110–11)
  Myidae (in part): softshell clams (pp. 104–5)

ELONGATE
Wing
  Pholadidae: piddock clams and angelwings
    (pp. 107–9)
  Veneridae (in part): venus clams
    (pp. 96–104)
Cigar
  Mytilidae (in part): mussels (pp. 34–40)
Razor
  Solecurtidae: stout razor clams (pp. 94–95)
  Solenidae: jackknife clams (p. 111)
  Solemyidae: awningclams (pp. 32–33)
Fan-Shaped
  Pinnidae: penshells (pp. 49–50)
  Mytilidae (in part): mussels (pp. 34–40)
  Pteriidae: pearl oysters (pp. 47–48)
  Gastrochaenidae: chimney clams, flask
    clams (pp. 113–14)

SMALL SHELL
POINTED POSTERIOR
  Nuculanidae: nutclams (p. 33)
  Pandoridae: pandora clams (pp. 114–15)
  Corbulidae (in part): corbula clams
    (pp. 105–7)
  Yoldiidae: yoldias (p. 34)

IRREGULAR/VARIABLE
Influenced by dense clustering or attachment
to substrate.
  Ostreidae: oysters (pp. 51–53)
  Plicatulidae: kittenpaws (p. 60)
  Anomiidae: jingle shells (pp. 54–56)
  Chamidae: jewelboxes (pp. 73–75)

They also are presented here as an aid to identification. Ultimate identifications should depend on good matches with photos and descriptions in individual species accounts.

BIVALVES

Principal Shell Characteristics to Examine

General shell shape and size.

Structure of hinge plate and hinge teeth (including ligament).

Definition and shape of muscle scars and pallial sinus.

Shell weight or thickness and sculptural features on the external surface.

Bivalve Hinge Plate and Hinge Tooth Structures

When identifying bivalves, paying attention to hinge plate and hinge teeth structures can be helpful. Check the illustrations for examples.

Taxodont teeth are a row of many similar small teeth on both sides of the beak, or umbones. These teeth interlock with a similar row in the opposite valve. Examples of specimens with taxodont teeth include ark shells (Arcidae, Noetiidae), bittersweet clams (Glycymerididae), and nutclams (Nuculidae, Nuculanidae).

Heterodont teeth are two to three strong triangular teeth centered under the umbones and interlocking with teeth in the opposite valve, usually with two elongate lateral teeth in the left valve, one in front and one behind the beak. These interlock into two pairs of lateral teeth in the right valve. These usually have a strong external ligament (as in Veneridae and Cardiidae), but in some families (Mactridae) the teeth are arranged around a cuplike depression in both valves in which the internal ligament is seated.

In some families (Mytilidae, Pinnidae, and Pteriidae) hinge teeth are very reduced or absent, with a strong external ligament.

In some species, small teeth, or tubercles, on either side of a small internal compressible ligament (or resilium) articulate with matching depressions or sockets in the opposing valve (isodont hinge). These include oysters (Ostreidae); scallops (Pectinidae); kittenpaws (Plicatulidae); and with a more prominent ball-and-socket hinge, thorny oysters (Spondylidae). Similar hinges, but

Bivalve Hinge Plate Structure and Hinge Teeth

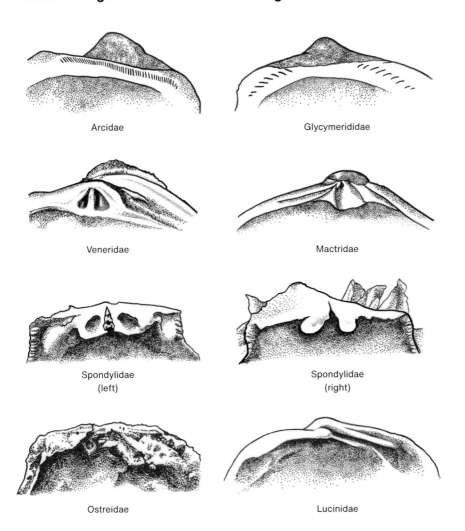

Arcidae

Glycymerididae

Veneridae

Mactridae

Spondylidae
(left)

Spondylidae
(right)

Ostreidae

Lucinidae

with more elongate teeth surrounding the internal ligament (crurae hinge), characterize the jingle shells (Anomiidae) and pandoras (Pandoridae).

GASTROPODS

Principal Shell Characteristics to Examine

General shell shape and size; presence/absence of siphonal canal.

Proportional lengths of spire, aperture, and siphonal canal regions.

Presence, character, and spacing of varices (earlier outer lips from when the shell was smaller).

Presence and character of teeth, notches, or folds on columella and/or outer lip.

Color patterns and sculptural features on the external surface of whorls.

CAP-SHAPED
Little or no spiral structure cap; wide-open on bottom.
  Fissurellidae: keyhole limpets (p. 118)
  Calyptraeidae: slippersnails
    Cup-and-Saucer (pp. 137–40)

TOP-SHAPED
No siphonal canal.
  Littorinidae: periwinkles (pp. 129–30)
  Turbinidae: turbans, starsnails
    (pp. 120–21)
  Calliostomatidae: topsnails (pp. 118–20)
  Xenophoridae: carriersnails (pp. 155–56)
  Architectonicidae: sundials (p. 197)

GLOBE-SHAPED
Large oval aperture; low spire.
  Naticidae: moonsnails (pp. 130–34)
  Epitoniidae (in part): janthinas
    (pp. 124–29)

Gastropod shapes guide.
Illustration by Georgia Minnich.
Courtesy of North Carolina Sea Grant.

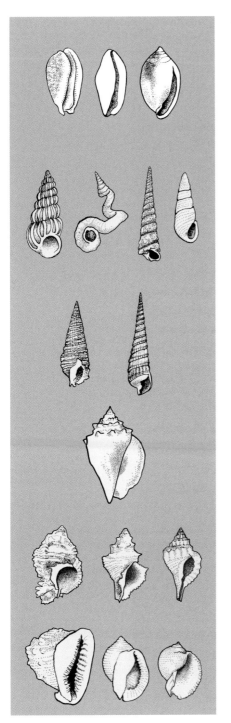

OVOID ELONGATE
Usually with inward reflected lip; long aperture, often with teeth on one or both lips.
    Cypraeidae: cowries (pp. 140–42)
    Ovulidae: simnias, cyphomas (pp. 142–43)
    Triviidae: trivias (pp. 143–44)
    Marginellidae: marginellas (pp. 156–57)
    Ellobiidae: melampi (pp. 201–22)

AUGER- OR TURRET-SHAPED
Very high spire; lacking siphonal canal.
    Epitoniidae (in part): wentletraps
       (pp. 124–29)
    Turritellidae: wormsnails, turretsnails
       (pp. 122–23)
    Pyramidellidae: pyrams, odostomes
       (pp. 199–201)
    Eulimidae: eulimas (pp. 135–37)

AUGER- OR TURRET-SHAPED
Very high spire, with short, open siphonal canal.
    Cerithiidae: ceriths/bittiums (pp. 121–22)
    Cerithiopsidae: miniature ceriths (p. 134)
    Terebridae: augers (pp. 195–96)

HEAVY, THICK SHELLS; SHORT SPIRE
Flared outer lip in adult shell; short upturned siphonal canal; curved notch at base of outer lip.
    Strombidae: true conchs (pp. 145–46)

HEAVY, THICK SHELLS; ROUND TO OVAL APERTURES
Straight, narrow siphonal canal; prominent axial sculpture, many with ornamental spines.
    Muricidae: drills, rocksnails, murexes
       (pp. 176–82)
    Coralliophilidae: coralsnails (pp. 182–83)

HELMET- OR CASK-SHAPED
Large globose body whorl; short siphonal canal.
    Cassidae: helmet shells, Scotch Bonnet
       (pp. 148–50)
    Tonnidae: tuns (p. 146)

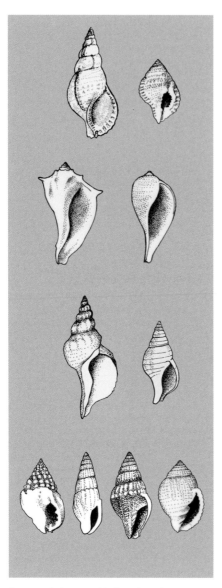

STRONG, THICKENED OUTER LIPS AND PROMINENT AXIAL RIBS
(Varices) that represent earlier outer lips.
Charoniidae: trumpet tritons (p. 151)
Cymatiidae: tritons (pp. 152–54)
Bursidae: frogsnails (p. 147)
Personidae: distorsios (pp. 154–55)

WHELK-SHAPED, LOW SPIRES
With apertures and long, tapered siphonal canals and columella; thin, smooth inner and outer lips; may be sinistral.
Busyconidae: whelks (pp. 160–64)
Ficidae: figsnails (pp. 144–45)

LARGE, SPINDLE-SHAPED
Oval aperture narrows into moderately long, straight siphonal canal.
Fasciolariidae: horse conch,
tulip snails (pp. 168–70)

SMALL TO MEDIUM, SPINDLE-SHAPED
Small apertures and short, sometimes toothed siphonal canal.
Nassariidae: mudsnails (pp. 170–74)
Columbellidae: dovesnails (pp. 165–67)
Colidae: Colus (pp. 164–65)
Pisaniidae: Cantharus (pp. 174–75)
Costellariidae: miters (pp. 182–83)
Cancellariidae: nutmegs (158–59)

Gastropod shapes guide (*continued*).
Illustration by Georgia Minnich.
Courtesy of North Carolina Sea Grant.

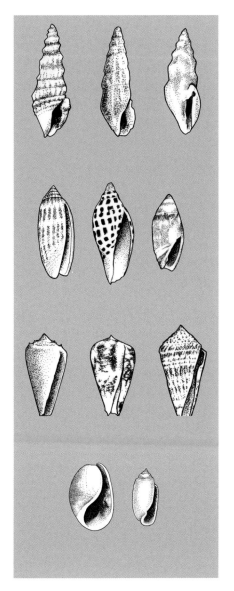

SMALL, SPINDLE-SHAPED

Prominent axial ribs, aperture less than half the shell length, and distinct notch or groove (turrid notch) at top of outer lip.
  Clathurellidae: oxias (pp. 190–91)
  Drilliidae: drillias (pp. 191–92)
  Mangeliidae: mangelias (pp. 192–94)
  Pseudomelatomidae: drillias (pp. 194–95)

OLIVE-SHAPED

Elongate cylindrical shells, very short siphonal canals at front of shell.
  Olividae: olives, olivellas (pp. 183–86)
  Volutidae: junonia (pp. 157–58)

CONE-SHAPED

Straight-sided with long, narrow, parallel-sided aperture opening at base of cone.
  Conidae: cone shells (pp. 186–89)

BUBBLE-SHAPED

Medium to small ovate/elongate shells, long aperture rounded at base; no siphonal canal.
  Bullidae: bubble shells (pp. 197–98)
  Tornatinidae: barrel-bubbles (pp. 198–99)

Species Descriptions
Bivalves

....

THE FOLLOWING LIST OF FAMILIES within the class Bivalvia found in North Carolina are arranged in taxonomic and phylogenetic order based on the work of Bieler, Carter, and Coan within a scientific paper by Bouchet et al. (2010). In the species description, shapes are often general due to the wide character variability within most molluscan families. See also the illustrations of general shell shapes for bivalves in the "How to Use This Guide" section.

Nuculidae	Gryphaeidae	Chamidae	Myidae
Solemyidae	Anomiidae	Basterotiidae	Corbulidae
Nuculanidae	Pectinidae	Cyrenoididae	Pholadidae
Yoldiidae	Spondylidae	Mactridae	Hiatellidae
Mytilidae	Plicatulidae	Anatinellidae	Solenidae
Arcidae	Limidae	Tellinidae	Pharidae
Glycymerididae	Lucinidae	Donacidae	Gastrochaenidae
Noetiidae	Carditidae	Semelidae	Pandoridae
Pteriidae	Crassatellidae	Solecurtidae	Lyonsiidae
Pinnidae	Arcticidae	Ungulinidae	Periplomatidae
Ostreidae	Cardiidae	Veneridae	

Bivalves by Family

NUCULIDAE (NUTCLAMS)

Shell small, rounded, pearly inside; "piano" hinge (series of teeth positioned next to one another like keys on a piano).

Atlantic Nutclam
Nucula proxima (Say, 1822)

DESCRIPTION: (¼ inch) Small, obliquely ovate shell with a shiny, smooth surface. Angular beak. Small, spoon-shaped depression under beak. Hinge line split into a 90-degree angle. Row of many crescent-shaped teeth on hinge. Inside of ventral edge crenulated or irregularly wavy. COLOR: Exterior and interior iridescent white to gray. HABITAT: Lives in sand near shore in moderate-salinity estuaries and offshore in depths of more than 100 feet. Commonly washed onto ocean beaches. RANGE: Nova Scotia, Canada, to Florida and Texas. NOTES: Also called a Common Nutclam and Near Nut Shell. It is often eaten by fish and frequently found in the stomach of the sea star *Astropecten articulatus.*

Atlantic Nutclam

SOLEMYIDAE (AWNINGCLAMS)

Fragile rectangular shell; tough, fringed, or rayed periostracum.

Atlantic Awningclam
Solemya velum (Say, 1822)

DESCRIPTION: (1 inch) Elongate, smooth, and fragile shell more than twice as long as high. Named for tough periostracum extending beyond the shell's edge as if it were an awning or fringe.

Atlantic Awningclam

Beak near one end. No teeth on hinge. Possibly some weak crenulations at ventral edge. COLOR: Brown exterior with radial rays appearing light beneath the dark brown periostracum. Grayish-white interior. HABITAT: Lives in sounds, burrowed into intertidal sand flats in U-shaped burrows. Rarely washed onto sound beaches. RANGE: Nova Scotia, Canada, to Florida. NOTES: Also known as the Veiled Clam. This animal has about 16 papillae on its siphon. It is an active swimmer. It should be stored carefully in collections because the awning is fragile. See plate 1.

NUCULANIDAE (NUTCLAMS)

Shell small, thin, elongate, not pearly inside; piano hinge (series of teeth positioned next to one another like keys on a piano); taxodont dentation.

Pointed Nutclam

Pointed Nutclam
Nuculana acuta (Conrad, 1831)

DESCRIPTION: (⅜ inch) Small, thick, elliptical shell with one rounded end and one acutely pointed end. Top edge of shell slightly concave on the pointed end. Surface covered with evenly spaced and sized concentric ridges. Hinge line a wide obtuse angle. Row of many chevron-shaped teeth on hinge. COLOR: Gray. HABITAT: Lives offshore on mud-sand bottoms in 50-foot depths. Occasionally found in high-salinity estuaries. Commonly washed onto ocean beaches. RANGE: Cape Cod, Massachusetts, to Texas and Brazil. NOTES: This species is frequently found in the stomach of the sea star *Astropecten articulatus*.

YOLDIIDAE (YOLDIAS)

Thin, not pearly inside; small; elongate; "piano" hinge (series of teeth positioned next to one another like keys on a piano); taxodont dentation.

File Yoldia
Yoldia limatula (Say, 1831)

DESCRIPTION: (1¼ inches) Similar to the **Pointed Nutclam** except much larger and with smooth rather than highly striated exterior. COLOR: Exterior whitish to chestnut gray to light greenish. Interior glossy white to tan. HABITAT: Lives off Beaufort Inlet at depths of 30 feet and more.

File Yoldia

Occasionally found on ocean beaches. RANGE: Nova Scotia, Canada, to south of Beaufort Inlet. NOTES: This species is sometimes confused with the Short Yoldia (*Yoldia sapotilla* [A. Gould, 1841]), which may have a similar habitat in North Carolina. The latter species is shorter and has a broadly rounded end instead of a pointed end.

MYTILIDAE (MUSSELS)

Narrow, fan shaped; beak near narrow end; inside pearly.

Atlantic Papermussel
Arcuatula papyria (Conrad, 1846)

DESCRIPTION: (1 inch) Elongate, fragile shell generally more than twice as long as high. Smooth exterior with fine concentric growth lines. COLOR: Shiny light blue and tan exterior

Atlantic Papermussel

with brown cobwebby design. Iridescent interior.

Light green periostracum. **HABITAT:** Lives in estuaries and offshore. **RANGE:** Maryland to Texas. **NOTES:** It uses its byssal threads to build nests. **SCIENTIFIC NAME CHANGE:** Previous name: *Amygdalum papyrium* (Conrad, 1846). The species has been reassigned to the genus *Arcuatula*.

....

Cinnamon Mussel

Botula fusca (Gmelin, 1791)

Cinnamon Mussel

DESCRIPTION: (½ inch) Small, oblong shell with concave lower edge. Strong concentric growth lines. Beak at one end sometimes appears to form a hook. No hinge teeth. Shiny periostracum. **COLOR:** Grayish brown to dark chestnut brown. **HABITAT:** Lives offshore, burrows into rocks and shells. **RANGE:** North Carolina to Brazil. **NOTES:** See **Scissor Datemussel** notes.

....

Scorched Mussel

Brachidontes exustus (Linnaeus, 1758)

Scorched Mussel

DESCRIPTION: (1½ inches) Small, elongate, fan-shaped shell. Narrow end not strongly hooked. Axial ribs on the surface. Beak toward one end. One to four small hinge teeth. **COLOR:** Brownish yellow–gray exterior. Whitish to shiny purplish-gray interior, splotched with reddish purple. Yellowish-brown periostracum. **HABITAT:** Lives in estuaries, often attached to oysters, other shells, or rocks. **RANGE:** North Carolina to Venezuela. **NOTES:** It is commonly washed ashore still attached to shells, rocks, and seaweed.

Ribbed Mussel

....

Ribbed Mussel
Geukensia demissa (Dillwyn, 1817)

DESCRIPTION: (5¼ inches) Elongate, obliquely oval shell with one end narrower than the other. Strong, heavy radial ribs sometimes branched. Toothless hinge. COLOR: Dark brown to purplish exterior. Blue-white interior. Olive brown to dark brown periostracum. HABITAT: Lives in large groups in muddy intertidal areas of brackish marshes. Often found in clusters among the roots of smooth cordgrass (*Spartina alterniflora*). RANGE: Nova Scotia, Canada, to Florida. NOTES: It attaches to cordgrass stems, roots, and other substrates by its byssus. It grows well in polluted areas.

Hooked Mussel

....

Hooked Mussel
Ischadium recurvum (Rafinesque, 1820)

DESCRIPTION: (1¾ inches) Curved, triangular shell with strong radial ribs that branch near one end. Narrow end of shell strongly hooked with beak near the end. A few toothlike crenulations on hinge. COLOR: Dark grayish-black exterior. Polished purple interior with white at margins. HABITAT: Lives in estuaries, often attached within clusters of oysters on pilings or rocks. RANGE: Massachusetts to the Caribbean. NOTES: Also called a Bent Mussel.

Scissor Datemussel

....

Scissor Datemussel
Leiosolenus aristatus (Dillwyn, 1817)

DESCRIPTION: (1¼ inches) Elongate, narrow shell, circular in cross-section. Extended posterior tips like crossed fingers, the end of a small pair of scissors, or sometimes an open bird's beak. COLOR: Light brown exterior generally covered by white calcareous deposit. HABITAT: Lives offshore, burrowed into coral lumps, soft rock, and thick shells. RANGE: North Carolina to Venezuela. NOTES: It bores into calcareous rocks and shells using a mildly acidic secretion to soften the substrate and then abrades the softened material away with its shell. It breathes and feeds through siphons that it extends outside of its burrow. SCIENTIFIC NAME CHANGE: Previous name: *Lithophaga aristata* (Dillwyn, 1817). The species has been reassigned to the genus *Leiosolenus*.

Mahogany Datemussel

....

Mahogany Datemussel
Leiosolenus bisulcatus (d'Orbigny, 1853)

DESCRIPTION: (1¼ inches) Oblong, cylindrical shell. Exterior surface divided by a strong oblique line from beak area to bluntly pointed posterior end of shell. Ends not crossed. Calcareous deposits on surface. COLOR: Light brown exterior with white calcareous deposits. HABITAT: Lives in sounds and offshore, burrowed inside coral and soft rock. RANGE: North Carolina to Brazil. NOTES: See **Scissor Datemussel** notes. SCIENTIFIC NAME CHANGE: Previous name: *Lithophaga bisulcata* (d'Orbigny, 1853). The species has been reassigned to the genus *Leiosolenus*.

Giant Datemussel

Giant Datemussel
Lithophaga antillarum (d'Orbigny, 1853)

DESCRIPTION: (3¼ inches) Cigar-shaped shell with rounded ends. Sculptured with many light, irregular, vertical lines. No hinge teeth. COLOR: Light yellow-brown exterior. Brown periostracum. HABITAT: Lives offshore (mainly off Cape Lookout) inside lumps of coral. RANGE: North Carolina to Brazil. NOTES: Planktonic larvae attach to limestone and other soft rocks by a byssus, and the juveniles bore into the substrate as they grow to adulthood. See **Scissor Datemussel** notes.

American Horsemussel

American Horsemussel
Modiolus americanus (Leach, 1815)

DESCRIPTION: (2¼ inches) Elongate, oblong, inflated shell. One end narrower than the other. Resembles **Northern Horsemussel** but not as large and heavy. No ribs on smooth exterior, only concentric growth lines. Rolled, pearly area just below its ligament. Stringlike, hairy periostracum. COLOR: Brown exterior, sometimes with reddish purple or pink. Deep chestnut splotch in lower anterior area. Grayish-white or reddish interior. Light brown periostracum. HABITAT: Lives in sounds and offshore, attached to rocks, shells, and jetties. Commonly found on ocean beaches after storms. RANGE: North Carolina to Brazil. NOTES: This species is also called Tulip Mussel because of the reddish color on its shell when dead.

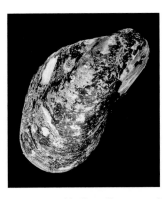

Northern Horsemussel

Northern Horsemussel
Modiolus modiolus (Linnaeus, 1758)

DESCRIPTION: (4½ inches) Elongate shell generally more than twice as long as high. Coarse concentric growth lines. Occasionally some radiating lines. Beak points toward one end. No hinge teeth. Leathery periostracum with some hairs. COLOR: No chestnut splotch on lower anterior area as in **American Horsemussel**. Pale purple to rose-white exterior. Brownish-black periostracum. HABITAT: Lives offshore, north of Cape Hatteras. Attaches to rocks and hard surfaces. Uncommonly found on ocean beaches north of Hatteras. RANGE: Arctic seas to Virginia and North Carolina. NOTES: This is the largest and most common mussel of New England, but it is not considered good to eat. It withstands waves by attaching to objects with a tough, elastic byssus. Its streamlined shape allows water to glide by with little resistance.

False Horsemussel

False Horsemussel
Modiolus squamosus (Beauperthuy, 1967)

DESCRIPTION: (2¼ inches) Lacks the rolled, pearly area below its ligament that is reported in the **American Horsemussel**. Flat triangular hairs on periostracum. COLOR: Similar to **Northern Horsemussel** and American Horsemussel. Chestnut splotch on lower anterior area not as showy as on the American Horsemussel. HABITAT: Occurs offshore and in high-salinity estuaries south of Cape Hatteras. Fairly common on jetties in Bogue Sound. RANGE: North Carolina to Venezuela. NOTES: Formerly a subspecies of, and easily confused with, Northern Horsemussel. SCIENTIFIC NAME CHANGE: Originally described as subspecies

Modiolus modiolus squamosus (Beauperthuy, 1967). *Modiolus squamosus* (Beauperthuy, 1967) is now accepted as a valid species.

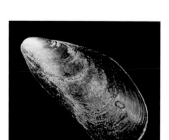

Blue Mussel

Blue Mussel
Mytilus edulis (Linnaeus, 1758)

DESCRIPTION: (2½ inches) Elongate, triangular shell generally twice as long as high. No radial ribs but many fine concentric lines. Beak located at one end of shell. Small teeth just under beak. Shiny periostracum. COLOR: Bluish-black exterior. White interior with lavender near edges. Young specimens sometimes greenish or rayed. HABITAT: Lives offshore and in mouths of estuaries, attached to rocks, shells, jetties, and pilings. Common on ocean beaches north of Cape Hatteras. Adults rarely found south of Cape Hatteras. RANGE: Arctic Ocean to South Carolina. NOTES: This is a popular edible mussel in Europe. It is smaller than most of North Carolina's other edible bivalves, but it may have potential for aquaculture. It withstands waves by attaching to hard surfaces by a tough, elastic byssus. Its streamlined shape allows water to glide by with little resistance.

ARCIDAE (ARK SHELLS)

Thick, heavy shells, with straight "piano" hinge (series of teeth positioned next to one another like keys on a piano); taxodont dentation. Frequently with residues of brown periostracum on the exterior surface. See also the family Noetiidae (false ark clams).

....

Incongruous Ark

Anadara brasiliana (Lamarck, 1819)

DESCRIPTION: (2½ inches) Inflated, rectangular shell with 26 to 28 strong radial ribs crossed by fine concentric lines. Grooves between ribs. Left valve distinctly larger than right. Ligament extends in anterior and back of beak. Straight hinge line with many chevron-shaped teeth, smaller toward the center. Ventral edge crenulated from strong exterior radial ribbing. **COLOR:** White. **HABITAT:** Lives buried in sand. Commonly found on ocean beaches. **RANGE:** North Carolina to Uruguay. **NOTES:** See **Ponderous Ark** notes.

Incongruous Ark

....

Cut-Ribbed Ark

Anadara secticostata (Reeve, 1844)

DESCRIPTION: (4½ inches) Large, sturdy, rectangular shell with 30 or more radial ribs, each with a fine groove running down the center. Prominent unbeaded ribs cut by fine concentric lines. Long, straight hinge line with many tiny, chevron-shaped teeth. Ventral edge crenulated. Mossy periostracum when alive. **COLOR:** Exterior white. Periostracum brown when alive. **HABITAT:** Lives offshore. Occasionally found on ocean beaches. **RANGE:** North Carolina to Texas. **NOTES:** Many of these arks were brought to shore by North Carolina's once-thriving **Atlantic Calico Scallop** fishery. See also **Ponderous Ark** notes. **SCIENTIFIC NAME CHANGE:** The name *Anadara floridana* (Conrad, 1869) is superseded by an earlier name, *Anadara secticostata* (Reeve, 1844).

Cut-Ribbed Ark

....

Transverse Ark
Anadara transversa (Say, 1822)

DESCRIPTION: (1 inch) Rectangular-shaped shell with 30 to 35 ribs. Ribs beaded (usually only on left valve) but not cut lengthwise by fine lines (as in the **Cut-Ribbed Ark**). Beak slightly off-center, nearer the anterior end. Ligament extends in anterior and back of beak. Straight hinge line with many chevron-shaped teeth. Hairy periostracum when alive. COLOR: White exterior and interior. Dark brown periostracum when alive.

Transverse Ark   HABITAT: Attaches to rocks, shells, and driftwood in sounds and inlets and offshore. Occasionally found on ocean beaches. RANGE: Massachusetts to Texas. NOTES: Its periostracum is usually worn away except around edge.

....

Turkey Wing
Arca zebra (Swainson, 1833)

DESCRIPTION: (3½ inches) Elongate shell with beak positioned well toward the anterior end and a sharp posterior ridge from the beak to the posterior edge. Ribs at rear not beaded. Straight hinge line with many small, chevron-shaped teeth. Resembles **Mossy Ark** except ventral edge is neither crenulated nor strongly concave. Live specimens often covered by a shaggy periostracum and/or encrusting organisms. COLOR: Yellowish-white or yellowish-brown exterior with reddish-brown zebra-stripe markings. Whitish to pale lavender interior. HABITAT: Attaches to shells or rocks on offshore fishing grounds or nearshore hard surfaces. Commonly found on ocean beaches. RANGE: North Carolina to Brazil. NOTES:

Turkey Wing

Also called a Zebra Ark. It attaches to objects by a byssus and is often difficult to see because of encrusting growths.

....

White-Beard Ark

White-Beard Ark

Barbatia candida (Helbling, 1779)

DESCRIPTION: (1 inch) Similar to the **Transverse Ark** but less rectangular. Anterior and posterior borders not parallel. Many fine, rough radial ribs crossed by concentric growth lines. Straight hinge line with many chevron-shaped teeth. Ventral edge crenulated from strong, exterior radial ribbing. Thin, shaggy periostracum when alive. COLOR: White exterior. Yellowish-brown periostracum when alive. HABITAT: Attaches with byssus to rocks. Occasionally found on ocean beaches. RANGE: North Carolina to Brazil. NOTES: Also called a Bright Ark. It attaches to rocks by byssal threads.

....

White Miniature Ark

Barbatia domingensis (Lamarck, 1819)

DESCRIPTION: (up to 1¼ inches but usually much smaller) Squarish, small, rough shell. Strong concentric ridges across weaker ribs. Long ligament. Long, almost straight hinge line with many tiny, chevron-shaped teeth. Ventral edge of shell not crenulated. COLOR: White to yellowish white. HABITAT: Attaches to offshore jetties and shells or under rocks. Occasionally found on ocean beaches. RANGE: North Carolina to Brazil. NOTES: Also called a Reticulate Ark. This bivalve has a bitter taste. It uses a byssus to attach to rocks and other hard objects.

White Miniature Ark

. . . .

Mossy Ark
Lamarcka imbricata (Bruguière, 1789)

DESCRIPTION: (2½ inches) Similar in shape to, and often confused with, **Turkey Wing** but with weaker ribs. Ribs generally beaded. Part of lower edge strongly concave. Straight hinge line with many chevron-shaped teeth. Shaggy periostracum when alive. COLOR: No exterior zebralike markings. White to pale, lavender interior. HABITAT: See Turkey Wing. RANGE: North Carolina to Brazil. NOTES: It attaches to objects by a byssus and is often difficult to see because of encrusting growths. SCIENTIFIC NAME CHANGE: Previous name: *Arca imbricata* (Bruguière, 1789). The species has been reassigned to the genus *Lamarcka*.

Mossy Ark

. . . .

Blood Ark
Lunarca ovalis (Bruguière, 1789)

DESCRIPTION: (2¼ inches) Oval-elliptical shell with 26 to 35 smooth radial ribs not crossed by strong bars (as in the **Incongruous Ark**). Ligament area behind beak. Straight hinge line with chevron-shaped teeth extending only slightly beyond beak. Ventral edge crenulated from strong exterior radial ribbing. COLOR: White exterior. Thick periostracum with greenish brown on lower portion when alive. HABITAT: Lives buried in sand and mud. Very commonly found on ocean beaches. RANGE: Massachusetts to Texas. NOTES: Named for its red blood (most mollusks have bluish blood), it is sometimes called a Bloody Clam. See also **Ponderous Ark** notes. SCIENTIFIC NAME CHANGE: Previous name: *Anadara ovalis* (Bruguière, 1789). The species has been reassigned to the genus *Lunarca*.

Blood Ark

GLYCYMERIDIDAE
(BITTERSWEET CLAMS)

Thick heavy shells, nearly circular in shape, with somewhat curved "piano" hinge (series of teeth positioned next to one another like keys on a piano); taxodont dentation.

Giant Bittersweet

Giant Bittersweet

Glycymeris americana (DeFrance, 1826)

DESCRIPTION: (4 inches) Round, somewhat flat shell. Indistinct broad radial ribs sculptured with radiating scratches. Central beak. Long, curved hinge with 19 to 24 teeth. Scalloped margin. No pallial sinus. Velvety periostracum. COLOR: Grayish-tan exterior, mottled with yellowish brown. Dark brown periostracum. HABITAT: Lives offshore. Dense concentrations at 75-foot depths off Cape Fear. Commonly found on beaches near and south of Cape Fear. Occasionally netted as incidental catch by offshore fishing boats. RANGE: North Carolina to Florida. NOTES: It has a bitter taste, as its name implies, so it cannot be considered for commercial harvest. It has a muscular foot.

Comb Bittersweet

Comb Bittersweet

Tucetona pectinata (Gmelin, 1791)

DESCRIPTION: (¾ inch) Round, somewhat flat shell. About 20 strong, smooth radial ribs crossed by tiny concentric lines. Curved hinge line with 22 to 25 teeth. No pallial sinus. COLOR: Grayish white to yellowish white with yellow or brown splotches. HABITAT: Lives in shallow and offshore waters in sand or mud. Commonly found on ocean beaches. RANGE: North Carolina to Brazil. NOTES: It has a bitter taste and a muscular foot. Two other species—the Spectral Bittersweet (*Glycymeris spectralis* [Nicol, 1952]) and the Wavy Bittersweet (*Glycymeris undata* [Linnaeus, 1758])—are found sporadically off the North Carolina coast. SCIENTIFIC NAME CHANGE: Previous name: *Glycymeris pectinata* (Gmelin, 1791). The species has been reassigned to the genus *Tucetona*.

NOETIIDAE (FALSE ARK CLAMS)

Thick shell; somewhat curved "piano" hinge (series of teeth positioned next to one another like keys on a piano); taxodont dentation.

Cancellate Ark

Cancellate Ark

Arcopsis adamsi (Dall, 1886)

DESCRIPTION: (½ inch) Small, rectangular shell. Similar to **White Miniature Ark** but crisscross sculpturing less coarse and ligament only a small bar-like area between beaks. Straight hinge line with many chevron-shaped teeth. Ventral edge smooth inside. Thin periostracum when living. COLOR: White to yellowish-white exterior. White

interior. Pale brown periostracum when alive.
HABITAT: Attaches to rocks. Occasionally found on
ocean beaches. RANGE: North Carolina to Brazil.
NOTES: It attaches to the underside of rocks by a
byssus. The Cancellate Ark was previously known
as the Adams' Ark.

....

Ponderous Ark
Noetia ponderosa (Say, 1822)

DESCRIPTION: (2½ inches) Square, heavy shell.
About 30 radial ribs cut by fine concentric lines
but not beaded. Long hinge line, narrower in
center with many chevron-shaped teeth. Wide
ligament cut by transverse lines (at 90-degree
angle to length of ligament). Ventral edge not
crenulated. Heavy, mossy periostracum when
alive. COLOR: White to yellowish white. Black

Ponderous Ark

periostracum when alive. HABITAT: Lives in inlets
and offshore, commonly found on ocean beaches.
RANGE: Virginia to Texas. NOTES: Its threadlike
byssus is lost during larval stages. During its
adult stage, it burrows in sand or mud rather
than attaching to objects.

....

PTERIIDAE (PEARL OYSTERS)

Irregular, lumpy shape, with winglike extension
of long, straight hinge line.

....

Atlantic Pearl-Oyster
Pinctada imbricata (Röding, 1798)

DESCRIPTION: (1½ inches) Nearly circular shell
with long, straight hinge line forming a small
winglike extension. Small, flattened ligament in

Atlantic Pearl-Oyster

center of hinge line. Byssal notch below small triangular ear of the right valve. Thin-shelled and brittle; often cracks when dry. Thin, scaly, concentric spines sometimes on periostracum. COLOR: Exterior yellow or green with dark radial streaks or dark brownish purple with white streaks. Pearly interior. HABITAT: Attaches to sea whips and other soft corals, sargassum, or other drifting objects. Often found on ocean beaches where sargassum washes ashore from the Gulf Stream. RANGE: North Carolina to Florida, Texas, and Brazil. NOTES: See **Atlantic Wing-Oyster** notes.

....

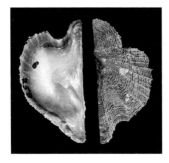

Atlantic Wing-Oyster

Atlantic Wing-Oyster
Pteria columbus (Röding, 1798)

DESCRIPTION: (3¾ inches) Triangular shell with winglike extension from the straight hinge line. Other side rounded. Hinge on longest part of shell with few teeth. Wrinkled exterior. COLOR: Brownish-purple exterior. Iridescent interior. HABITAT: Lives in high-salinity sounds and offshore, commonly attached to shells, rocks, sea whips, or floating docks. Often found on sea whips washed ashore after storms. Occasionally found on sound and ocean beaches. RANGE: North Carolina to Brazil. NOTES: It rarely produces pearls, and when it does, they are usually too small to be commercially valuable. The mantle produces mother-of-pearl, or nacre. Pearls form when a grain of sand or other particle enters the shell and is coated with layers of nacre. See plate 2.

PINNIDAE (PENSHELLS)

Large, fan-shaped shells; thin and brittle, with radial ribs, some with spines.

Stiff Penshell

Stiff Penshell

Atrina rigida ([Lightfoot], 1786)

DESCRIPTION: (10 inches) Large, fragile, fan-shaped shell. Fewer than 20 ribs, some with large spines. One side straight and the other rounded. Distinguished from **Half-Naked Penshell** by position of large muscle scar, which in this species borders the outside edge of the nacreous area. COLOR: Dark purplish-black exterior. Pearly interior. HABITAT: Lives in sounds and offshore. Found on sound and ocean beaches after winter storms. RANGE: North Carolina to Florida. NOTES: Also called Rigid Penshell. See **Sawtooth Penshell** notes. See the photograph for an outline of the muscle scar and nacreous area on the left valve.

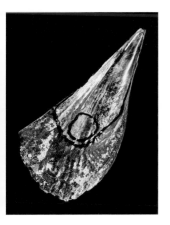

Half-Naked Penshell

Half-Naked Penshell

Atrina seminuda (Lamarck, 1819)

DESCRIPTION: (10 inches) Nearly identical to **Stiff Penshell** except on mid-interior of shell. Large muscle scar is completely surrounded by nacreous area, which extends to the narrow beak end of the shell. (On Stiff Penshell, large muscle scar is on the edge of nacreous area.) COLOR: Dark purplish-black exterior. Pearly interior. HABITAT: Lives offshore in sandy mud. Occasionally found on ocean beaches after winter storms. RANGE: North Carolina to Argentina. NOTES: See **Sawtooth Penshell** notes. See the photograph for an outline of the muscle scar and nacreous area.

....

Sawtooth Penshell
Atrina serrata (G. B. Sowerby I, 1825)

DESCRIPTION: (10 inches) Large and fan-shaped shell with one side straight and the other rounded. Fragile and scaly. About 30 ribs covered with small spines. **COLOR:** Green to yellowish-brown exterior. Pearly interior. **HABITAT:** Lives offshore in sandy mud. Commonly found on ocean beaches after winter storms. **RANGE:** North Carolina to Colombia. **NOTES:** Brittleness makes this shell difficult to keep in collections. Its edible meat is considered valuable in some parts of the world. Penshell adductor muscle is sometimes sold under the name scallop. Byssal threads, which help hold it in the sand, are woven into cloth for small garments in Mediterranean countries. Penshells are the only shellfish in North Carolina's marine waters known to produce a valuable pearl.

Sawtooth Penshell

....

Amber Penshell
Pinna carnea (Gmelin, 1791)

DESCRIPTION: (11 inches) Narrow, thin shell with radial ridge in the middle of the valve. May have several rows of scalelike spines. **COLOR:** Amber to light orange. **HABITAT:** Lives offshore in sandy or mud-sand areas. The pointed end is buried deeply, with byssal threads attached to stones or shells. **RANGE:** Offshore Cape Hatteras to Florida; Texas; Caribbean to Brazil. **NOTES:** A typically Caribbean species, found by scuba divers near shipwrecks off Cape Hatteras.

Amber Penshell

OSTREIDAE (OYSTERS)

Irregular, lumpy shape; porcelain-like shell.

Eastern Oyster

Eastern Oyster

Crassostrea virginica (Gmelin, 1791)

DESCRIPTION: (8½ inches) Shell elongate and usually heavy. Shaped by the surface to which it attaches (usually another oyster). Lacks pimple-like depressions on either side of hinge and lacks hinge teeth. Prominent muscle scar inside. Lower valve cemented to another hard surface. COLOR: Dirty white to dark gray or purple exterior. Grayish-white interior with dark purple muscle scar. HABITAT: Lives in intertidal areas near mouths of sounds and estuaries. Common on sound and ocean beaches. RANGE: New Brunswick, Canada, to the Gulf of Mexico. NOTES: The Eastern Oyster is an important fishery in North Carolina's estuarine waters. It may change sex several times during its life. It sheds sperm and eggs into water, where fertilization and development take place. Larvae swim freely for about two weeks, cement to a hard object, and remain for life. For a brief period after attachment, they are called spat. Thousands of spat have been recorded attached to one oyster shell, but generally only one or two will survive. The mantle does not produce nacre, or mother-of-pearl, so pearls found in Eastern Oysters are not valuable. They are sometimes called Coon Oysters when they grow long, narrow, and thin-shelled, under crowded conditions in intertidal areas.

Frond Oyster

....

Frond Oyster
Dendostrea frons (Linnaeus, 1758)

DESCRIPTION: (1½ inches) Irregular radial ridges on surface create sharply scalloped edges. Series of clasping projections on one of the radial ridges on lower valve. No hinge teeth. Pimple-like depressions on the inside edges of valve near the beak. COLOR: Red to purplish brown. HABITAT: Lives offshore, usually attached to sea whips. Collected by scuba divers at 100-foot depths in Cape Fear region. Rarely found on ocean beaches. RANGE: North Carolina to Florida and Brazil. NOTES: Also sometimes called a Coon Oyster. It attaches to sea whips with clasping projections.

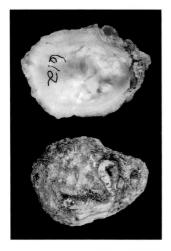

Crested Oyster

....

Crested Oyster
Ostrea equestris (Say, 1834)

DESCRIPTION: (2 inches) Shell very similar to (small) **Eastern Oyster** but usually rounder and with near-microscopic pimple-like protrusions on either side of hinge plate in upper valve and matching (interlocking) tiny dimple-like depressions on opposite valve. More convex side of hinge often with distinctly higher, finely crenulated edge. COLOR: Brownish-gray exterior. Greenish-gray interior. Muscle scar generally not colored. HABITAT: Lives in high-salinity areas, such as mouths of sounds, estuaries, and offshore. Common on sound and ocean beaches. RANGE: Virginia to Argentina. NOTES: Rarely used commercially, it is only an incidental catch from high-salinity sounds or inlets. It has an excellent taste and is closely related to commercial oysters in Europe and on the northwestern US coast. Unlike the Eastern Oyster, which releases eggs and sperm into the water, sperm enter the female's mantle cavity through her incurrent siphon. The fertilized eggs of the Crested Oyster are incubated within the mantle until they hatch and are released into surrounding waters. In both species, the young develop similarly regardless of sex, and sex reversal is common. **SCIENTIFIC NAME CHANGE:** Previous name: *Ostreola equestris* (Say, 1834). The species has been reassigned to the genus *Ostrea*.

....

Sponge Oyster

Sponge Oyster
Ostrea permollis (G. B. Sowerby II, 1871)

DESCRIPTION: (2 inches) Similar to **Crested Oyster**. Small, roundish shell with pointed or twisted beak. Both valves flat. Wrinkled surface somewhat soft. No hinge teeth. One muscle scar. Ligament often angled down from the beak. Some round pimple-like depressions on inner edges. Lower valve cemented to another hard surface. **COLOR:** Yellowish-orange exterior with a silky sheen. White to dark gray interior. **HABITAT:** Lives offshore, usually embedded in round sponge masses (*Stellata* species) in 80-to-100-foot depths south of Cape Lookout. Also reported to live under rock slabs. Found by scuba divers and netted as incidental catch by fishing trawlers. Sponge masses occasionally washed onto ocean beaches. **RANGE:** North Carolina to Florida and the Caribbean. **NOTES:** Related to the Crested Oyster, and females incubate the young. **SCIENTIFIC NAME CHANGE:** Previous name: *Cryptostrea permollis* (G. B. Sowerby II, 1871). The species has been reassigned to the genus *Ostrea*.

GRYPHAEIDAE (OYSTERS)

Valves strongly unequal; lumpy shape;
chalky interior.

Foam Oyster

Foam Oyster

Hyotissa mcgintyi (H. W. Harry, 1985)

DESCRIPTION: (3½ inch) Robust shell, more or
less circular in outline, irregularly sculptured
externally, can have wavy, zigzag, saw-toothed
margin. If the valve were broken, a honeycomb-
like internal structure would be revealed. COLOR:
Cream (when small) to white/lavender as adults.
HABITAT: Hardbottom substrata, including rocks,
other shells, and shipwrecks. RANGE: Includes the
tropical eastern and western Atlantic, extending
into the northern Gulf of Mexico and to North
Carolina. NOTES: Hugh Porter sent specimens
collected by the Institute of Marine Sciences east-
southeast of Cape Fear at 250-to-600-foot depths
to H. W. Harry in 1981 for identification, and they
formed the basis of Harry's 1985 species description for establishing the species' range northward
into North Carolina. Additional North Carolina
specimens have since been recovered from a
beached navigational buoy.

ANOMIIDAE (JINGLE SHELLS)

Irregular, lumpy circular shape, thin, translucent,
and shiny; lower (right) valve has hole for byssal
attachment and rarely washes ashore.

Common Jingle

·········

Common Jingle
Anomia simplex (d'Orbigny, 1853)

DESCRIPTION: (1½ inches) Irregularly oval or round shell, thin and almost translucent. Top valve more convex. Bottom valve flat and fragile with a slot-like hole near the hinge. One large and several small muscle scars close together. No hinge teeth. **COLOR:** Exterior top (convex) valve whitish to yellow orange to silvery black. Translucent bottom (flat) valve. Pearly interior. **HABITAT:** Lives from the low-tide line to shallow offshore waters, attached but not cemented to rocks, oysters, and other hard surfaces. Upper (left) valves commonly found on sound and ocean beaches. **RANGE:** New York to the Caribbean. **NOTES:** A large byssus protrudes through the hole in its lower valve and attaches to other objects. The top shell often takes the appearance of the shell it attaches to. These shells are sometimes strung up and used as wind chimes.

Prickly Jingle

·········

Prickly Jingle
Heteranomia squamula (Linnaeus, 1758)

DESCRIPTION: (¾ inch) Similar to **Common Jingle** but much smaller, with tiny spines on upper valve. One large muscle scar above two smaller muscle scars on bottom valve. **COLOR:** Exterior opaque whitish tan. Interior shiny purplish white. **HABITAT:** Lives in high-salinity estuaries and offshore waters, attached but not cemented to hard surfaces such as stones, shells, or floating objects (buoys). Occasionally found on ocean beaches. **RANGE:** Labrador, Canada, to North Carolina. **NOTES:** See Common Jingle notes. **SCIENTIFIC NAME CHANGE:** Previous name: *Anomia squamula* (Linnaeus, 1758). The species has been reassigned to the genus *Heteranomia*.

Atlantic Falsejingle

·········

Atlantic Falsejingle
Pododesmus rudis (Broderip, 1834)

DESCRIPTION: (1¼ inches) Thin, fragile, oval to round shell. Surface roughened by fine irregular riblets, primarily near valve edges. Right valve cemented to the substrate with a large hole for the byssus. One large and one small muscle scar on inside of the other valve. COLOR: Cream exterior. Interior may have some brownish purple near the muscle scars. HABITAT: Lives offshore. Found attached to ark shells and bittersweet clams at 100-foot depths in the Cape Fear area. Collected by scuba divers from metal rubble of sunken shipwrecks south of Cape Lookout. Rarely found on ocean beaches. RANGE: North Carolina to Texas and Brazil. NOTES: Also called a False Jingleshell.

···

PECTINIDAE (SCALLOPS)

Broadly rounded, nearly circular, usually with two large ears forming a straight hinge line.

Atlantic Calico Scallop

·········

Atlantic Calico Scallop
Argopecten gibbus (Linnaeus, 1758)

DESCRIPTION: (3 inches) Similar in shape and sculpturing to the **Bay Scallop**. Both valves cupped. Hinge line with ears. About 20 radial ribs sometimes roughened by growth lines. COLOR: Exterior of upper (left) valve dark yellow or pink with striking combinations of red in stripes or blotches. Lower (right) valve whitish with small reddish or purple spots. White interior, often with brown patches on ears and top edge. HABITAT: Lives only in the ocean, east of Cape Lookout and southwest of Beaufort Inlet in 100-foot depths.

Commonly found on sound and ocean beaches.
RANGE: Delaware to Brazil. **NOTES:** Occasionally
fished commercially. This shell is popular among
beachcombers.

....

Bay Scallop

Bay Scallop
Argopecten irradians concentricus (Say, 1822)

DESCRIPTION: (3½ inches) Similar in shape and
sculpturing to **Atlantic Calico Scallop** (but note
color differences). Both valves cupped; 15 to 22
smooth radial ribs. **COLOR:** Upper valve gray,
brown, or blackish, sometimes with only the
upper surface of ribs colored. Lower valve usually
with less color than the upper valve. **HABITAT:** In
North Carolina, lives only in sounds and estuaries.
RANGE: Massachusetts to Mexico. **NOTES:** At times
a commercial fishery in North Carolina sounds
and estuaries, it is often associated with eelgrass
beds. The loss of eelgrass, however, has caused a
decline in the Bay Scallop here. See plate 3.

....

Round-Rib Scallop

Round-Rib Scallop
Euvola raveneli (Dall, 1898)

DESCRIPTION: (2¾ inches) Hinge line with ears.
Lower valve very cupped; upper valve flat. Smooth,
radial ribs with wide spaces between them. **COLOR:**
Pinkish, purple, or sometimes yellow. Upper valve
darker with irregular dark markings. **HABITAT:**
Lives offshore. **RANGE:** North Carolina to the
Caribbean. **NOTES:** This scallop was once mistaken
by shellfishers for a sick **Atlantic Calico Scallop**
because of its flat upper valve. Because it rarely
washes ashore, the flat valve is a unique find for
beachcombers. **SCIENTIFIC NAME CHANGE:** Previous
name: *Pecten raveneli* (Dall, 1898). The species has
been reassigned to the genus *Euvola*.

Rough Scallop

Rough Scallop

Lindapecten muscosus (W. Wood, 1828)

DESCRIPTION: (1¾ inches) Small, scallop-shaped shell. About 20 strong ribs with many erect scales or small spines near the margin. Straight hinge line with ears. COLOR: Pink to dark red exterior, occasionally mixed with other colors. Sometimes bright lemon yellow. HABITAT: Lives offshore. Rarely found on ocean beaches. RANGE: North Carolina to the Caribbean. NOTES: It was frequently netted as incidental catch in the **Atlantic Calico Scallop** fishery. See plate 4.

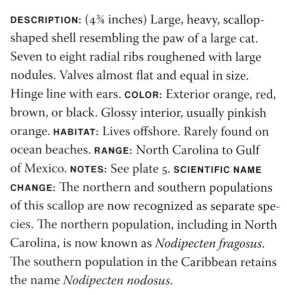

Northern Lions-Paw Scallop

Northern Lions-Paw Scallop

Nodipecten fragosus (Conrad, 1849)

DESCRIPTION: (4¾ inches) Large, heavy, scallop-shaped shell resembling the paw of a large cat. Seven to eight radial ribs roughened with large nodules. Valves almost flat and equal in size. Hinge line with ears. COLOR: Exterior orange, red, brown, or black. Glossy interior, usually pinkish orange. HABITAT: Lives offshore. Rarely found on ocean beaches. RANGE: North Carolina to Gulf of Mexico. NOTES: See plate 5. SCIENTIFIC NAME CHANGE: The northern and southern populations of this scallop are now recognized as separate species. The northern population, including in North Carolina, is now known as *Nodipecten fragosus*. The southern population in the Caribbean retains the name *Nodipecten nodosus*.

Sea Scallop

Sea Scallop
Placopecten magellanicus (Gmelin, 1791)

DESCRIPTION: (6½ inches) Large, smooth shell. Hinge line with ears. Many fine concentric lines. Lower valve almost flat, and upper valve only slightly inflated. **COLOR:** Exterior of top valve reddish brown, sometimes rayed; bottom valve glossy pinkish white. Whitish interior. **HABITAT:** Lives offshore north of Cape Hatteras. Might occur on ocean beaches north of Cape Hatteras. **RANGE:** Labrador, Canada, to Cape Hatteras. **NOTES:** Also called the Atlantic Deep-Sea Scallop, it is fished commercially for its delicious meat. It grows much larger than other North Carolina scallops. Specimens from Virginia and New Jersey were once common in piles near commercial scallop-shucking plants in Carteret County. Early Native Americans used the valves as dishes.

SPONDYLIDAE (THORNY OYSTERS)

Lower (right) valve convex, heavy, with smaller spines, and attached to hard substrate; upper valve nearly flat with radiating rows of spines, small ears, and ball-and-socket hinge teeth.

Atlantic Thorny Oyster

Atlantic Thorny Oyster
Spondylus americanus (Hermann, 1781)

DESCRIPTION: (4 inches) Large, thick, broadly ovate shell with radiating rows of long, thin spines. Length of spines highly variable, from short to more than 2 inches long. May resemble a jewelbox externally, but this shell has ears like a scallop, a ball-and-socket hinge, and a central ligament. COLOR: White or cream exterior with yellow to pink, red, or purple. White interior. HABITAT: Lives on rocks and shipwrecks in offshore waters more than 60 feet deep. RANGE: Cape Hatteras to Florida, Texas, and Brazil. NOTES: It attaches by its right valve to hard surfaces. The spines grow longer in quiet water. Worn left valves occasionally wash ashore. See plate 6.

....

PLICATULIDAE (KITTENPAWS)

Irregular, lumpy shape; radial ridges resemble a cat's outstretched paw.

....

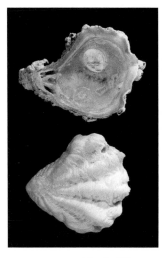

Atlantic Kittenpaw
Plicatula gibbosa (Lamarck, 1801)

DESCRIPTION: (1½ inches) Small, thick, fan-shaped shell resembling the outstretched paw of a kitten. Six or seven rounded radial ribs or folds. Two strong hinge teeth in upper wave fit into sockets of the lower valve. One muscle scar. Lower valve cemented or showing signs of having been cemented to a hard surface. COLOR: Whitish-gray exterior with reddish-brown lines. Whitish interior. HABITAT: Lives offshore, cemented to shell or rock. Commonly found on ocean beaches. RANGE: North Carolina to Argentina. NOTES: Shell colors fade quickly, so most beach specimens are dull white to gray.

Atlantic Kittenpaw

LIMIDAE (FILECLAMS)

Broad, oval, scallop-shaped shell with prickly surface; hinge has two small ears.

Rough Fileclam
Ctenoides scaber (Born, 1778)

DESCRIPTION: (2⅝ inches) Compressed, oval-shaped shell with small ears. Coarse radial ribbing resembles narrow roof shingling. Gap on one side of shell. Long tentacles when alive. COLOR: Whitish exterior but thin, brown periostracum lends it a brownish color. White interior. Bright orange-red mantle and tentacles when alive.

Rough Fileclam

HABITAT: Lives offshore, attached to rocks and shipwrecks. Collected by scuba divers at depths greater than 75 feet. RANGE: Cape Hatteras to Florida, Texas, and Brazil. NOTES: Also called a Rough Lima or Atlantic Rough File Shell. The animal attaches to surfaces by its byssus but also swims in a manner similar to scallops by opening and closing its valves. Another form of this species, *Ctenoides mitis* (Lamarck, 1807), is smoother and has finer, more numerous ribs. SCIENTIFIC NAME CHANGE: Previous name: *Lima scabra* (Born, 1778). The species has been reassigned to the genus *Ctenoides*.

Antillean Fileclam
Limaria pellucida (C. B. Adams, 1848)

DESCRIPTION: (¾ inch) Oval-elongate, inflated shell. Many fine radial ribs of uneven sizes on surface. Small, straight hinge line. Ears almost equal in length. Under ears a long, narrow gape in the front and large gape in the back. Thin-shelled.

Antillean Fileclam

COLOR: Translucent to yellowish white. HABITAT: Lives in high-salinity estuaries, such as Bogue Sound, Newport River, and North River, usually attached to the substrate. Also found offshore at depths down to 100 feet. RANGE: North Carolina to Florida, Texas, and Brazil. NOTES: Also called an Antillean Lima or Inflated File Shell. It is known to surround itself with a nest of byssal threads. It is able to swim in a manner similar to scallops. SCIENTIFIC NAME CHANGE: Previous name: *Lima pellucida* (C. B. Adams, 1846). The species has been reassigned to the genus *Limaria*.

LUCINIDAE (LUCINE CLAMS)

Shells nearly circular with long, narrow muscle scar; greatly reduced or no pallial sinus.

Buttercup Lucine

Buttercup Lucine
Anodontia alba (Link, 1807)

DESCRIPTION: (2¾ inches) Rounded, plump shell. Smooth exterior except for fine concentric sculpture. Indistinct hinge teeth. Long muscle scar on inside. No pallial sinus. COLOR: Dull white exterior with bright yellowish orange on the sides. Interior tinged with yellow to orange. HABITAT: Lives in shallow to offshore waters. Occasionally washed onto ocean beaches. RANGE: North Carolina to the Caribbean. NOTES: See **Cross-Hatched Lucine** notes. A very similar species, the Chalky Buttercup Lucine (*Pegophysema philippiana* [Reeve, 1850]) is found uncommonly on North Carolina beaches. That species is larger (3½ inches) and more deeply convex, and the interior surface is dimpled (rough) and usually white to gray.

Dosinia Lucine

Dosinia Lucine
Callucina keenae (Chavan, 1971)

DESCRIPTION: (¾ inch) Disklike shell with many fine concentric ridges on the surface. Ridges are cut by finer radial lines, especially near the beak and anterior edge. Moderately high beak points over a submerged lunule. Inside edge often lightly crenulated. Weak lateral and strong cardinal teeth on hinge. No pallial sinus. COLOR: White. HABITAT: Known living in 50-to-100-foot depths offshore of Beaufort Inlet. Collected by divers from 40 feet. RANGE: North Carolina to Florida and the Caribbean. SCIENTIFIC NAME CHANGE: Previous name: *Lucina keenae* (Chavan, 1971). The species has been reassigned to the genus *Callucina*.

Cross-Hatched Lucine

Cross-Hatched Lucine
Divalinga quadrisulcata (d'Orbigny, 1846)

DESCRIPTION: (¾ inch) Small, rounded plump shell. Pattern of tiny grooves swirls around surface, resulting in a chevron-like sculpture. Hinge teeth. Crenulations on inside edges. No pallial sinus. COLOR: White. HABITAT: Lives in shallow to offshore water. Common on ocean beaches. RANGE: Massachusetts to Brazil. NOTES: Shells are often used in crafts. SCIENTIFIC NAME CHANGE: Previous name: *Divaricella quadrisulcata* (d'Orbigny, 1846). The species has been reassigned to the genus *Divalinga*.

Pennsylvania Lucine

......

Pennsylvania Lucine

Lucina pensylvanica (Linnaeus, 1758)

DESCRIPTION: (2½ inches) Round, thick shell with delicate to strong concentric ridges on outer surface. Pronounced furrow from beak to back ventral edge of the shell. Well-marked lunule with a raised center. Cardinal and lateral hinge teeth present. No pallial sinus but well-marked pallial line. On recently living specimens, the thin periostracum may be ridged concentrically outward and flaked off easily. COLOR: White exterior and interior. Yellow periostracum. HABITAT: Known living in sand offshore of Core Banks and Cape Fear. Rarely found on ocean beaches. RANGE: North Carolina to Florida and Brazil. NOTES: The large size allows it to wash ashore occasionally. SCIENTIFIC NAME CHANGE: Previous name: *Linga pensylvanica* (Linnaeus, 1758). The species has been reassigned to the genus *Lucina*.

Woven Lucine

......

Woven Lucine

Lucinisca nassula (Conrad, 1846)

DESCRIPTION: (½ inch) Moderately compressed, disklike shell. Rough, reticulated surface often with raised scales at the juncture of concentric and radial lines. Moderately high beak with small pit in front. Strong lateral and cardinal teeth on hinge. No pallial sinus. Strongly crenulated inside edge. COLOR: White. HABITAT: Known living off Beaufort Inlet at depths from 30 to 100 feet. Occasionally washed onto ocean beaches. RANGE: North Carolina to Florida, Texas, and the Bahamas. SCIENTIFIC NAME CHANGE: Previous name: *Lucina nassula* (Conrad, 1846). The species has been reassigned to the genus *Lucinisca*.

Many-Line Lucine

....

Many-Line Lucine

Parvilucina crenella (Dall, 1901)

DESCRIPTION: (⅜ inch) Small, circular, robust shell with low ridge from the prominent beak to the back ventral edge of the shell. Sculptured surface with many incised concentric lines crossed by many finely incised radial lines. Cardinal and lateral teeth on hinge. Small and smooth lunule. Ventral edge of shell crenulated. No pallial sinus. COLOR: White. HABITAT: Lives in moderate-to-high-salinity estuaries and offshore (common in 50-foot depths and occasionally in 100-foot depths). Commonly washed onto ocean beaches. RANGE: Virginia to Florida and Brazil. NOTES: This species is often found in the stomach of the sea star *Astropecten articulatus*. SCIENTIFIC NAME CHANGE: Previous name, *Parvilucina multilineata* (Tuomey and Holmes, 1857), refers to an extinct (fossil) species. The replacement name for the recent species is *Parvilucina crenella* (Dall, 1901).

CARDITIDAE (CARDITA CLAMS)

Small, round, slightly triangular shell, with prominent pointed beak; no pallial sinus; broad radial ribs; strong cardinal tooth in one valve.

Threetooth Carditid

....

Threetooth Carditid

Pleuromeris tridentata (Say, 1826)

DESCRIPTION: (¼ inch) Small, chunky triangular shell of equal height and length. Strongly beaded radial ribs. Central beak. One strong, triangular cardinal hinge tooth under beak of the right valve; two slightly smaller diverging cardinal teeth on the left valve. Inside edge of shell strongly crenulated. No pallial sinus. COLOR: Cream to pinkish-gray exterior. Creamy white to red interior. HABITAT: Lives on sandy and shelly bottoms offshore to about 75-foot depths and in high-salinity estuaries. Commonly found on ocean beaches south of Cape Hatteras. RANGE: Cape Hatteras to Florida. NOTES: The holes on the shell in the photograph are the result of predatory activity by a moonsnail.

Flattened Carditid

Flattened Carditid

Pteromeris perplana (Conrad, 1841)

DESCRIPTION: (⅜ inch) Small, somewhat flattened, obliquely oval, or triangular shell. Beak back of center. Strong, broad, rough radial ribs that curve toward anterior of the shell. Ribs sometimes beaded. Hinge teeth similar to those of **Three-tooth Carditid**. Inside edge of shell crenulated. No pallial sinus. COLOR: Creamish exterior with occasional pink concentric bands. Cream interior with occasional pink to strong violet. HABITAT: Lives in 20-to-30-foot depths south of Cape Hatteras. Occasionally found on ocean beaches. RANGE: North Carolina to Florida. SCIENTIFIC NAME CHANGE: Previous name: *Pleuromeris perplana* (Conrad, 1841). The species has been reassigned to the genus *Pteromeris.*

CRASSATELLIDAE (CRASSATELLA CLAMS)

Two very distinctly shaped and different-sized species in North Carolina, both with thick shells, two cardinal teeth, and concentric ridges on surface.

....

Lunate Crassinella

Crassinella lunulata (Conrad, 1834)

DESCRIPTION: (¼ inch) Small, solid, flat, somewhat triangular shell. Top edge straight but diverges from the beak at a sharp 90-degree angle. About 15 to 20 low, sharp, concentric ribs on surface. COLOR: Cream to pink exterior, sometimes with brownish rays. Interior mostly brown. HABITAT: Lives in sandy, shell-hash bottoms in high-salinity estuaries and offshore down to depths greater than 100 feet. Commonly found on ocean beaches. RANGE: Massachusetts to Florida, Texas, and Brazil.

Lunate Crassinella

....

Beautiful Crassatella

Kalolophus speciosus (A. Adams, 1854)

DESCRIPTION: (2½ inches) Thick shell with one end rounded and the other pulled out to form a blunt, squarish extension. Closely spaced, heavy concentric ridges on surface. Beak near center. Two deep muscle scars on inside. No pallial sinus. COLOR: Brown exterior. Interior usually pinkish. HABITAT: Lives offshore. Occasionally brought in by **Atlantic Calico Scallop** fishers as incidental catch. RANGE: North Carolina to the Caribbean. NOTES: Also called Gibb's Clam. SCIENTIFIC NAME CHANGE: Previous name: *Eucrassatella speciosa* (A. Adams, 1854). The species has been reassigned to the genus *Kalolophus*.

Beautiful Crassatella

ARCTICIDAE (OCEAN QUAHOG)

A family with only one living species. Oval shells, like venus clams, but lacking lunule and pallial sinus. Specimens have been aged at 400 to 500 years, making them among the longest-lived animals known.

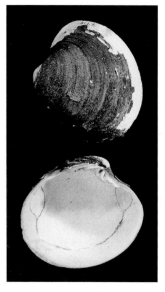

Ocean Quahog

Ocean Quahog
Arctica islandica (Linnaeus, 1767)

DESCRIPTION: (4½ inches) Heavy shell similar in shape and size to the **Northern Quahog** but has no lunule or pallial sinus. Fine crenulations on ventral edge. Periostracum coarse, shiny, and wrinkled. COLOR: Whitish exterior usually with dark brown or black periostracum. White interior. HABITAT: Lives offshore in beds of sandy mud. RANGE: Newfoundland, Canada, to Cape Hatteras. NOTES: It is also called a Mahogany Clam or Black Clam. A delicious species, it is not as popular as other clams, probably due to the orange color of its meat. It is fished commercially in New England and New Jersey.

CARDIIDAE (COCKLES)

Round to oval heart-shaped shells with central beak pointing upward; no lunule; no pallial sinus; two hooked cardinal teeth in each valve; narrow radial ribs or smooth eggshell-like surface.

··········

Atlantic Strawberry-Cockle

Americardia media (Linnaeus, 1758)

DESCRIPTION: (1½ inches) Thickish shell with squared-off posterior side. Strong radial ribs with no spines or elevated scales. Beak somewhat central. Strong tingle from beak to ventral edge. Prominent lateral teeth on hinge. Smooth interior. No pallial sinus. Ventral edge crenulated. COLOR: Creamy white exterior with irregular transverse rows of reddish-brown spots. Purplish spots sometimes in interior. HABITAT: Lives offshore. Occasionally found on ocean beaches. RANGE: North Carolina to Brazil. NOTES: See **Yellow Prickly Cockle** notes.

Atlantic Strawberry-Cockle

··········

Yellow Prickly Cockle

Dallocardia muricata (Linnaeus, 1758)

DESCRIPTION: (1¾ inches) Circular to oval, inflated shell with 30 to 40 radial ribs. Smooth ribs on center of shell; ribs on sides of shell with small, solid, non-scalelike spines over less than half the rib width. Ventral edge crenulated. Prominent lateral teeth on hinge. COLOR: Creamy white exterior with brown or red splotches. White and yellow interior. HABITAT: Occasionally lives in es-tuaries. Found on ocean beaches. More common south of Morehead City. RANGE: North Carolina to Argentina. NOTES: Cockles are commonly eaten in Europe. The animal has a long, powerful foot that allows it to actively move about. SCIENTIFIC NAME CHANGE: Previous name: *Trachycardium muricatum* (Linnaeus, 1758). The species has been reassigned to the genus *Dallocardia*.

Yellow Prickly Cockle

Atlantic Giant Cockle

....

Atlantic Giant Cockle
Dinocardium robustum ([Lightfoot] 1786)

DESCRIPTION: (4½ inches) Circular to ovate shell, thick and deeply inflated. Radial ribs rough but no spines or elevated scales. Beak somewhat central. Prominent lateral teeth on hinge. Ribbed interior. No pallial sinus. COLOR: Yellowish-white to pale rosy-brown exterior with bands of reddish brown or purplish spots. Rose to brown interior, paler toward anterior and darker toward rear. HABITAT: Lives in sounds and shallow offshore waters. Commonly found on sound and ocean beaches. RANGE: Virginia to Belize. NOTES: Its reddish meat makes an excellent chowder. It is the largest cockle on the Atlantic coast. See plate 7.

....

Yellow Eggcockle
Laevicardium mortoni (Conrad, 1831)

DESCRIPTION: (¾ inch) Small shell very similar to **Painted Eggcockle** except more rounded in shape. Eggshell-like surface with light or no ribbing. No pallial sinus. Beak somewhat central. Prominent lateral teeth on hinge. COLOR: Yellowish-white exterior, usually streaked with orange. Interior usually vivid yellow but fades quickly. HABITAT: Lives in sounds and estuaries. Occasionally found on sound beaches. RANGE: Massachusetts to Guatemala. NOTES: The Yellow Eggcockle was previously known as the Morton Eggcockle. See **Yellow Prickly Cockle** notes.

Yellow Eggcockle

Painted Eggcockle

. . . .

Painted Eggcockle

Laevicardium pictum (Ravenel, 1861)

DESCRIPTION: (1 inch) Small shell very similar to **Yellow Eggcockle** except flatter and more obliquely triangular in shape. Eggshell-like surface with light or no ribbing. No pallial sinus. Beak somewhat central. Prominent lateral teeth on hinge. COLOR: Creamy white exterior with strong brown splotches or zigzag bars. Yellow interior. HABITAT: Lives offshore. Rarely found on ocean beaches. RANGE: North Carolina to Brazil. NOTES: Previously known as Ravenel's Eggcockle. See **Yellow Prickly Cockle** notes.

Eggcockle

. . . .

Eggcockle

Laevicardium serratum (Linnaeus, 1758)

DESCRIPTION: (2¾ inches) Ovate to almost round, inflated, thin shell. Eggshell-like surface with light radial ribbing. No pallial sinus. Beak some-what central. Prominent lateral teeth on hinge. COLOR: Cream with brown tints. HABITAT: Lives in sand or mud, from shallow water to 150-foot depths offshore. Commonly found on ocean beaches. RANGE: North Carolina to Brazil. NOTES: See **Yellow Prickly Cockle** notes. This shell fades quickly to white on the beach. SCIENTIFIC NAME CHANGE: Previous name, *Laevicardium laevigatum* (Linnaeus, 1758), has been shown to be an Indo-Pacific species. The replacement name in the western Atlantic is *Laevicardium serratum* (Linnaeus, 1758).

Spiny Papercockle

Spiny Papercockle
Papyridea soleniformis (Bruguière, 1789)

DESCRIPTION: (1½ inches) Thin, elliptical shell slightly elongated and not deeply cupped. Radial ribs with tiny spines near their ends. Prominent lateral teeth on hinge. No lunule or pallial sinus. COLOR: Exterior and interior pinkish white, mottled with brownish orange and pink. HABITAT: Lives in high-salinity sounds and offshore. Its short siphons indicate that it lives just below the mud surface. Occasionally found on ocean beaches from Cape Lookout south. RANGE: North Carolina to Brazil. NOTES: See **Yellow Prickly Cockle** notes.

Florida Prickly Cockle

Florida Prickly Cockle
Trachycardium egmontianum (Shuttleworth, 1856)

DESCRIPTION: (3 inches) Oval, inflated shell uniformly covered by ribs, each bearing strong, prickly scales over more than half its length. Beak somewhat central. Prominent lateral teeth on hinge. No pallial sinus. Ventral edge crenulated. COLOR: Creamy white exterior, sometimes with brown or purple splotches. Interior salmon, vivid pink and purple. HABITAT: Lives near mouths of estuaries and in shallow offshore waters. Occasionally found on sound and ocean beaches. RANGE: North Carolina to Florida. NOTES: See **Yellow Prickly Cockle** notes. The shell is often used in crafts. See plate 8.

CHAMIDAE (JEWELBOXES)

Irregular, lumpy shape; thick shell; leafy or spiny ridges; one or both valves deeply cupped. Members of the genus *Chama* cement their lower cupped valve to a hard substrate, and only the flatter top valve is likely to appear on the beach.

Florida Spiny Jewelbox
Arcinella cornuta (Conrad, 1866)

DESCRIPTION: (2 inches) Thick shell pitted with six to eight strong radial ribs bearing prominent tubular spines. Surface between ribs beaded. Curved beak. Hinge teeth. Both valves deeply cupped, with prominent lunules. Adults not cemented to any hard surface. COLOR: White exterior. White interior with some pinkish red. HABITAT: Lives offshore. Occasionally found on ocean beaches. RANGE: North Carolina to Texas. NOTES: The young attach to small bits of shell or rock. Later they become free and lie on the bottom, but the smooth attachment scar remains visible in anterior of the beak on the right valve.

Florida Spiny Jewelbox

Corrugate Jewelbox
Chama congregata (Conrad, 1833)

DESCRIPTION: (1¼ inches) Small, heavy shell irregularly oval or rounded. Surface sculpture of low, wavy radial cords or ridges. Hinge teeth. Beak points toward right. Lower valve quite cupped and attached to hard surface. Upper valve a semiflat lid. COLOR: White exterior usually mottled with brown or reddish purple. Interior usually reddish. HABITAT: Lives offshore, attached to shells or

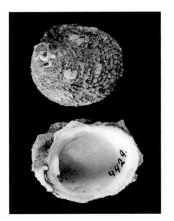

Corrugate Jewelbox

rocks. Occasionally found on ocean beaches.
RANGE: North Carolina to Brazil. NOTES: It is often
covered with algae.

....

Leafy Jewelbox
Chama macerophylla (Gmelin, 1791)

DESCRIPTION: (1½ inches) Solid, nearly circular,
oyster-like shell with leafy, ruffly, and sometimes
spiny sculpture usually noticeably arranged in
concentric pattern on upper shell. Strong, curved
hinge teeth. Beak in lower, attached valve points
toward right, or clockwise. Lower valve cupped
and always attached to hard surface. Upper
valve nearly flat, like a jewel box lid for the lower
valve. COLOR: Whitish exterior and interior with
variable but often brilliant colors such as yellow,
purple, orange, and pink. HABITAT: Lives offshore,
attached to shells and rocks. Upper (unattached)
valve rarely found on ocean beaches. RANGE:
North Carolina to Brazil. NOTES: The "ruffles"
grow larger in quiet waters.

Leafy Jewelbox

....

Atlantic Jewelbox
Pseudochama cristella (Lamarck, 1819)

DESCRIPTION: (2½ inches) Almost a mirror image
of **Leafy Jewelbox**, with beak pointing left, or
counterclockwise. Hinge teeth. Lower valve deeply
cupped and attached to hard surface. Upper valve
is a semiflat lid. COLOR: Exterior dull white to
dull, rusty red. Whitish interior often tinged with
brown. HABITAT: Lives in deep, offshore waters, attached to shells and rocks. Rarely found on ocean
beaches. RANGE: North Carolina to Brazil. NOTES:

Atlantic Jewelbox

Also called a Left-Handed Jewelbox. SCIENTIFIC
NAME CHANGE: Previous name, *Pseudochama
radians* (Lamarck, 1819), is preempted by the
original combination name *Pseudochama cristella*
(Lamarck, 1819).

....

BASTEROTIIDAE (SOFTSHELLS)

Small, rectangular shape; no hinge teeth or
external ligament; no pallial sinus.

....

Subovate Softshell

Subovate Softshell

Paramya subovata (Conrad, 1845)

DESCRIPTION: (⅜ inch) Small, somewhat rectangular shell with rough concentric lines on surface.
Beak slightly swollen and just off-center. Triangular depression on hinge with a single raised
cardinal tooth in each valve. The major identifying
mark is the noticeable extension of the triangular depression into the shell cavity. COLOR: Gray.
HABITAT: Lives offshore at depths up to 75 feet,
on muddy bottoms in the burrows of the marine
spoon worm *Thalassema hartmani*, both of which
are thought to depend on each other for their
survival. Commonly found on ocean beaches.
RANGE: Delaware to Florida and Texas. NOTES:
This species has been variously assigned to several
different families, most recently (2017), based on
DNA studies, to Basterotiidae. Only two species
of *Paramya* are currently recognized; *Paramya
africana* (Cosel, 1995) is a sister species found on
the west coast of tropical Africa.

....

CYRENOIDIDAE (MARSHCLAMS)

Round to oval shell, with heavy, dark periostracum, frequently with eroded area near beaks. Found only in low-salinity estuaries.

....

Carolina Marshclam

Carolina Marshclam

Polymesoda caroliniana (Bosc, 1801)

DESCRIPTION: (3¼ inches) Oval to rounded shell with concentric lines. Corroded areas common on exterior. Distinguished from **Atlantic Rangia**, with which it may be found, by darker periostracum and lack of triangular or spoon-shaped cavity in the hinge. COLOR: Light olive-brown exterior. Interior white but not polished. Dark brown to black periostracum. HABITAT: Lives in muddy sand and marshes of low-salinity areas near river mouths where its habitat may overlap with Atlantic Rangia and with freshwater mussels (Unionidae). RANGE: North Carolina to Texas. NOTES: The acids in brackish marshes cause the shell's surface to corrode. *Corbicula fluminea* (O. F. Müller, 1774), the introduced and invasive Asian Clam, in the closely related family Cyrenidae, is a common, strictly freshwater resident in most North Carolina rivers.

....

MACTRIDAE (SURFCLAMS)

Oval-shaped shell; hinge has prominent spoon-shaped depression (where the internal ligament is seated between the two pairs of lateral teeth).

Fragile Surfclam

....

Fragile Surfclam

Mactrotoma fragilis (Gmelin, 1791)

DESCRIPTION: (3¾ inches) Oval-shaped shell with broadly rounded ends. Smooth surface with many fine concentric lines. Thin, lightweight shell with two radial ridges on its back slope. Central beak. Broad pallial sinus almost under beak. Lunule absent. Ligament enclosed by triangular depression in hinge. Lateral teeth present as strong, thin plates. Absence of fine transverse grooves on lateral teeth distinguishes small specimens from small **Atlantic Surfclams**. **COLOR:** White exterior and interior. Yellowish periostracum. **HABITAT:** Lives in sounds and shallow offshore waters. Occasionally found on sound and ocean beaches. **RANGE:** North Carolina to Brazil. **NOTES:** See **Smooth Duckclam** notes. **SCIENTIFIC NAME CHANGE:** Previous name: *Mactra fragilis* (Gmelin, 1791). The species has been reassigned to the genus *Mactrotoma*.

Dwarf Surfclam

....

Dwarf Surfclam

Mulinia lateralis (Say, 1822)

DESCRIPTION: (¾ inch) Small, rounded, thin shell. Resembles a small **Atlantic Rangia** but lives in saltier estuaries. Smooth exterior with fine concentric lines; one radial ridge with tiny hairs runs down the more pointed end of the shell. Bulbous beak is almost central and points forward. Small, spoon-shaped cavity in hinge area. Young of this species are distinguished from young **Atlantic Surfclams** by absence of fine inner transverse grooves on lateral hinge teeth. **COLOR:** Light brown to ivory exterior. Whitish interior. Yellow periostracum. HABITAT: Common in estuaries with higher salinities than those containing Atlantic Rangia (more likely to be associated with **Eastern Oysters**). Common on sound and ocean beaches. RANGE: Maine to Texas. NOTES: Also called a Duckclam. Many marine fish and ducks depend on this clam for food. It lives just below the sediment surface and has two short, united siphons. Young are free-swimming, and sexes are separate.

. . . .

Atlantic Rangia

Atlantic Rangia
Rangia cuneata (G. B. Sowerby I, 1832)

DESCRIPTION: (3¼ inches) Thick, rounded, triangular shell shaped somewhat like a quahog's. Triangular cavity in hinge area. One end rounded and the other bluntly pointed and sloping. Frequently, periostracum attached. Young of this species distinguished from **Dwarf Surfclam** by absence of hairy ridge along the back slope of the shell. COLOR: Grayish-white exterior. Shiny white interior. Dark gray-brown periostracum. HABITAT: Lives commonly in low-salinity to almost freshwater areas of Albemarle and Croatan Sounds and the Neuse and Pamlico Rivers. Sometimes found living in large beds. Common on low-salinity sound beaches. RANGE: Virginia to Texas. NOTES: Also called a Wedge Rangia, this species may be confused with the **Carolina Marshclam**. Atlantic Rangia has a heavier shell and a polished interior. A small, local commercial rangia fishery was based on the Neuse River population in the mid-1970s, but the population was soon depleted.

PLATE 1. Atlantic Awningclam (*Solemya velum*)   PLATE 2. Atlantic Wing-Oyster (*Pteria colymbus*)

PLATE 3. Bay Scallop (*Argopecten irradians concentricus*)

PLATE 4. Rough Scallop (*Lindapecten muscosus*)

PLATE 5. Northern Lions-Paw Scallop (*Nodipecten fragosus*)

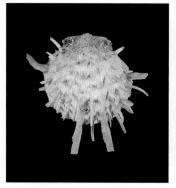

PLATE 6. Atlantic Thorny Oyster (*Spondylus americanus*)

PLATE 7. Atlantic Giant Cockle (*Dinocardium robustum*)

PLATE 8. Florida Prickly Cockle (*Trachycardium egmontianum*)

PLATE 9. Shiny Dwarf-Tellin (*Eurytellina nitens*)

PLATE 10. Great Tellin (*Laciolina magna*)

PLATE 11. Variable Coquina (*Donax variabilis*)

PLATE 12. Sunray Venus
(*Macrocallista nimbosa*)

PLATE 13. Calico Clam (*Megapitaria maculata*)

PLATE 14. Eastern Turretsnail (*Turritella exoleta*)

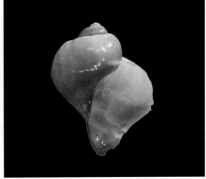

PLATE 15. Angulate Wentletrap (*Epitonium angulatum*)

PLATE 16. Elongate Janthina (*Janthina globosa*)

PLATE 17. Brown-Line Niso (*Niso aeglees*)

PLATE 18. Atlantic Deer Cowrie (*Macrocypraea cervus*)

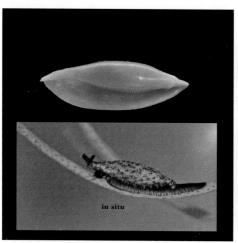

in situ

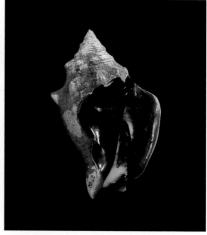

PLATE 19. One-Tooth Simnia (*Simnialena uniplicata*)

PLATE 20. Florida Fighting Conch (*Strombus alatus*)

PLATE 21. Giant Tun (*Tonna galea*)

PLATE 22. Cameo Helmet (*Cassis madagascariensis*)

PLATE 23. Clench Helmet
(*Cassis madagascariensis spinella*)

PLATE 24. Reticulate Cowrie-Helmet
(*Cypraecassis testiculus*)

PLATE 25. Scotch Bonnet (*Semicassis granulata*)

PLATE 26. Atlantic Trumpet Triton (*Charonia variegata*)

PLATE 27. Krebs' Hairy Triton (*Monoplex krebsii*)

PLATE 28. Seaboard Marginella (*Prunum roscidum*)

PLATE 29. Junonia
(*Scaphella junonia*)

PLATE 30. Knobbed Whelk
(*Busycon carica*)

PLATE 31. Channeled Whelk
(*Busycotypus canaliculatus*)

PLATE 32. Banded Tulip (*Cinctura hunteria*)

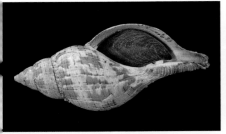

PLATE 33. True Tulip (*Fasciolaria tulipa*)

PLATE 34. Ribbed Cantharus (*Hesperisternia multangulus*)

PLATE 35. Giant Eastern Murex (*Hexaplex fulvescens*)

PLATE 36. Florida Rocksnail (*Stramonita floridana*)

PLATE 37. Lettered Olive (*Oliva sayana*)

PLATE 38. Variable Dwarf Olive (*Olivella mutica*)

PLATE 39. Largilliert's Cone (*Conus largillierti*)

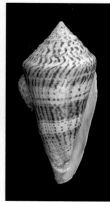

PLATE 40. Sozon's Cone (*Conasprella delessertii*)

PLATE 41. Simpson Drillia (*Lissodrillia simpsoni*)

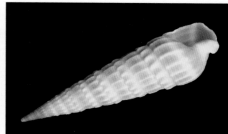

PLATE 42. Eastern Auger (*Neoterebra dislocata*)

PLATE 43. Greater Argonaut (*Argonauta argo*)

Southern Surfclam

Southern Surfclam
Spisula raveneli (Conrad, 1832)

DESCRIPTION: (2½ inches) Similar to **Atlantic Surfclam** but shell lower in height and beak less bulbous. COLOR: Yellowish or grayish-white exterior. Dull white interior. Light brown periostracum. HABITAT: Lives offshore in 10-to-30-foot depths. Commonly found near Cape Lookout and beaches south. RANGE: North Carolina to Texas. NOTES: This species gradually replaces the Atlantic Surfclam south of the Virginia border. Specimens up to 4 or 5 inches long have been found north of Cape Lookout. The common name Southern Surfclam replaces Ravenel Surfclam. SCIENTIFIC NAME CHANGE: Described previously as subspecies *Spisula solidissima raveneli* (Conrad, 1832). *Spisula raveneli* (Conrad, 1832) is now accepted as a valid species.

Atlantic Surfclam
Spisula solidissima (Dillwyn, 1817)

DESCRIPTION: (4¼ inches) Triangular shell with rounded ends. Smooth exterior with fine concentric lines. Triangular depression in hinge area just below the beak, which is almost central. Lateral teeth present as strong, thin plates with fine, inner transverse grooves. Narrow pallial sinus not extending under beak. No lunule. COLOR: Yellowish or grayish-white exterior. Dull white interior. Olive-brown periostracum. HABITAT: Lives offshore in beds north of Cape Hatteras. Frequently washed onto ocean beaches after storms. RANGE: Nova Scotia, Canada, to South Carolina. NOTES: Also called the Beach Clam, Skimmer Clam, Hen Clam, or Bar Clam. Except for penshells and the

Atlantic Surfclam

rare geoduck, it is the largest common bivalve on North Carolina beaches. Harvested commercially along the New Jersey coast, it has sustained the nation's largest molluscan fishery for many years.

....

ANATINELLIDAE (DUCKCLAMS)

Shell thin, oval shaped, one end rounded, the other narrow and pointed; hinge has triangular depression similar to Mactridae.

....

Smooth Duckclam

Smooth Duckclam

Anatina anatina (Spengler, 1802)

DESCRIPTION: (2¾ inches) Similar to the **Channeled Duckclam** but more elongate with fine, rather than strong, concentric lines. Distinct rib on back slope of shell. Thin-shelled. Lateral teeth not prominent. Ligament enclosed by triangular depression. COLOR: Cream exterior and interior. HABITAT: Lives in shallow offshore waters. Not as common on ocean beaches as the Channeled Duckclam. RANGE: North Carolina to Brazil. NOTES: It burrows just below the surface and has two short, united siphons. The sexes are separate, and young are free-swimming. May be confused with **Fragile Surfclam**.

....

Channeled Duckclam

Raeta plicatella (Lamarck, 1818)

DESCRIPTION: (2¾ inches) One end of oval shell bluntly pointed; other end broad and rounded. Shell thin, with strong rounded concentric ridges. Lateral teeth not prominent. Ligament enclosed by triangular depression in hinge. **COLOR:** Pure white exterior and interior. **HABITAT:** Lives in sand. Occasionally found on ocean beaches. **RANGE:** North Carolina to Argentina. **NOTES:** It lives just below the surface of the sand and has two short, united siphons. The sexes are separate, and young are free-swimming.

Channeled Duckclam

TELLINIDAE (TELLIN CLAMS)

Oval to round shape; thin-shelled; laterally compressed, usually with a slight twist at the posterior end; prominent external ligament behind tiny umbones; two cardinal teeth, sometimes no lateral teeth.

....

Northern Dwarf-Tellin

Ameritella agilis (W. Stimpson, 1857)

DESCRIPTION: (½ inch, but usually smaller) Small, elliptical shell with a rounded anterior end and a shorter, sloping back end. Beak behind the center. Smooth surface with microscopic, concentric threads that are strongest over the back shoulder area. Large pallial sinus almost touching anterior muscle scar. Right valve hinge with one lateral and one cardinal tooth; left valve hinge with one cardinal but no lateral tooth. **COLOR:** Front of exterior shiny to iridescent creamy white, occasionally with pinkish tints. Interior white. **HABITAT:** Lives

Northern Dwarf-Tellin

in mud flats of moderate-to-high-salinity estuaries. Less commonly lives offshore to depths of 75 feet or more. Common on ocean beaches. **RANGE:** Gulf of Saint Lawrence, Canada, to Georgia. **SCIENTIFIC NAME CHANGE:** Previous name: *Tellina agilis* (W. Stimpson, 1858). The species has been reassigned to the genus *Ameritella*.

....

Matagorda Macoma

Matagorda Macoma
Ameritella mitchelli (Dall, 1895)

DESCRIPTION: (¾ inch) Somewhat oblong, almost wedge-shaped shell. Lower edge almost flat and not as rounded as in the **Atlantic Macoma**. Concentric growth lines. Beak not quite central and not bulbous. Hinge with cardinal teeth only. **COLOR:** Dull white exterior. **HABITAT:** Lives in estuaries at salinities greater than those where the **Atlantic Rangia** thrives. Less common in estuarine rivers and sounds than the Atlantic Macoma. Occasionally found on sound beaches. **RANGE:** Virginia to Texas. **NOTES:** See Atlantic Macoma notes. The common name Matagorda Macoma replaces Mitchell's Macoma. **SCIENTIFIC NAME CHANGE:** Previous name: *Macoma mitchelli* (Dall, 1895). The species has been reassigned to the genus *Ameritella*.

....

Slandered Tellin

Slandered Tellin
Ameritella probrina (Boss, 1964)

DESCRIPTION: (⅜ inch) Elongated oval to almost rectangular, compressed shell. Fragile. Weak, irregularly spaced, concentrically incised lines on surface. No radial lines. Anterior edge of shell concave; back edge broadly rounded with a flat, oblique truncation. Typical *Tellinidae* teeth on hinge. Pallial sinus well separated from the anterior adductor muscle scar. **COLOR:** Shiny white exterior. Periostracum may make the surface iridescent. **HABITAT:** Lives offshore south of Cape Hatteras from depths of 30 to 60 feet or more. Occasionally washed onto ocean beaches. **RANGE:** North Carolina to Florida and Texas. **NOTES:** Also called Boss' Dwarf-Tellin. **SCIENTIFIC NAME CHANGE:** Previous name: *Tellina probrina* (Boss, 1964). The species has been reassigned to the genus *Ameritella*.

....

Sybaritic Tellin

Sybaritic Tellin
Ameritella sybaritica (Dall, 1881)

DESCRIPTION: (⅜ inch) Small, elongate, tellin-shaped shell somewhat thickened and not strongly compressed. Front of top edge long and slightly convex; back of top edge short and slightly concave. Ventral edge convex. Closely spaced, strongly incised lines on surface. Typical *Tellinidae* teeth on hinge. Pallial sinus approaches anterior muscle scar but then turns down to merge with the pallial line. **COLOR:** Exterior white to watermelon red. **HABITAT:** Lives offshore in sand south of Cape Hatteras from depths of 30 to 100 feet or more. Occasionally washed onto ocean beaches. **RANGE:** North Carolina to Florida and Brazil. **NOTES:** Also called Dall's Dwarf-Tellin. **SCIENTIFIC NAME CHANGE:** Previous name: *Tellina sybaritica* (Dall, 1881). The species has been re-assigned to the genus *Ameritella*.

Many-Colored Tellin

Many-Colored Tellin

Ameritella versicolor (De Kay, 1843)

DESCRIPTION: (½ inch) Similar to **Northern Dwarf-Tellin** except more elongate with a steeply sloping back edge and a flat ventral edge. Strongly incised concentric lines on surface spaced widely and evenly. These lines strong on the back slope of the right valve. Typical *Tellinidae* teeth on hinge. Pallial sinus close to the anterior muscle scar and partly attached to it. COLOR: Exterior shiny, iridescent white to red, frequently marked with radial rays of white to red. HABITAT: Lives offshore in sand to about 100-foot depths and occasionally in high-salinity estuaries. Occasionally washed onto ocean beaches. RANGE: Rhode Island to Florida, Texas, and the Caribbean. NOTES: Also called De Kay's Dwarf-Tellin. SCIENTIFIC NAME CHANGE: Previous name: *Tellina versicolor* (De Kay, 1843). The species has been reassigned to the genus *Ameritella*.

Alternate Tellin

Alternate Tellin

Eurytellina alternata (Say, 1822)

DESCRIPTION: (2½ inches) Solid, elliptical shell (longer than high), quite compressed. Subcentral beak. Many fine but prominent concentric lines. Shell round in front and more angular in back. COLOR: Shiny white exterior, sometimes pinkish or yellowish. White interior. Yellowish periostracum. HABITAT: Lives in shallow and offshore waters. Frequently washed onto ocean beaches. RANGE: North Carolina to Brazil. NOTES: Also called a Lined Tellin. It feeds on bottom detritus, burrows deep into the sand and has a long siphon. About 16 tellins are known in North Carolina off the coast and in the estuaries. All are much smaller than the Alternate Tellin except the **Great Tellin**, which may reach 5 inches long. **SCIENTIFIC NAME CHANGE:** Previous name: *Tellina alternata* (Say, 1822). The species has been reassigned to the genus *Eurytellina*.

....

Shiny Dwarf-Tellin

Shiny Dwarf-Tellin
Eurytellina nitens (C. B. Adams, 1845)

DESCRIPTION: (1½ inches) Almost identical in shape and sculpture to **Alternate Tellin** but smaller with weaker growth lines and different color. **COLOR:** Reddish orange. **HABITAT:** Lives offshore. Frequently brought up from the **Atlantic Calico Scallop** beds. **RANGE:** North Carolina to Texas and Brazil. **NOTES:** See plate 9. **SCIENTIFIC NAME CHANGE:** Previous name: *Tellina nitens* (C. B. Adams, 1845). The species has been reassigned to the genus *Eurytellina*.

....

Great Tellin

Great Tellin
Laciolina magna (Spengler, 1798)

DESCRIPTION: (5 inches) Large shell. Both ends slope to rounded margin with back end more pointed. Strong hinge with cardinal and lateral teeth. Smooth surface marked by growth lines. Pallial sinus. **COLOR:** Exterior of left valve white; exterior of right valve yellowish or orange. Interior often pinkish. **HABITAT:** Lives offshore. **RANGE:** North Carolina to the Caribbean. **NOTES:** Rare. Sought by collectors. See plate 10. **SCIENTIFIC NAME CHANGE:** Previous name: *Tellina magna* (Spengler, 1798). The species has been reassigned to the genus *Laciolina*.

Atlantic Macoma

Atlantic Macoma
Macoma petalum (Valenciennes, 1821)

DESCRIPTION: (1 inch) Small, oval to round, almost wedge-shaped shell. Many fine concentric lines. Central beak not bulbous. Thin-shelled. Hinge with cardinal teeth only. **COLOR:** Dull pinkish-white exterior. Shiny white interior. Olive-brown periostracum on bottom portion of shell. **HABITAT:** Lives commonly on mud bottoms in low-to-mid-salinity areas, such as coastal creeks, rivers, and sounds (coincident with *Rangia cuneata*). Occasionally found on sound beaches. **RANGE:** Bay of Fundy, Canada, to Georgia. **NOTES:** A deposit feeder, it burrows into mud and has a long incurrent siphon and a short excurrent siphon. The name Atlantic Macoma replaces Baltic Macoma. **SCIENTIFIC NAME CHANGE:** Previous name, *Macoma balthica* (Linnaeus, 1758), refers to an Arctic and eastern Atlantic species. The replacement name for the species in the western Atlantic is *Macoma petalum* (Valenciennes, 1821).

Elongate Macoma

Elongate Macoma
Macoploma tenta (Say, 1838)

DESCRIPTION: (¾ inch) Elliptical, elongate shell with a smooth surface. Beak slightly back from center. Back end of shell slightly twisted and narrower than the anterior end. No lateral teeth on hinge, but two narrow cardinal teeth on right valve and one cardinal tooth on left valve. Large pallial sinus. **COLOR:** Iridescent white exterior. Gray periostracum. **HABITAT:** Lives primarily in moderate-to-high-salinity estuaries. Occasionally found offshore to depths of about 100 feet. Sometimes found on sound and ocean beaches. **RANGE:**

Prince Edward Island, Canada, to Florida and Brazil. **NOTES:** Also called a Narrowed Macoma or Tenta Macoma. **SCIENTIFIC NAME CHANGE:** Previous name: *Macoma tenta* (Say, 1834). The species has been reassigned to the genus *Macoploma*.

....

Rainbow Tellin

Rainbow Tellin

Oudardia iris (Say, 1822)

DESCRIPTION: (½ inch) Small shell, shaped similarly to the **Many-Colored Tellin** but distinguished by surface sculpture. On this shell, concentric lines are cut angularly by microscopic lines (appropriately called sissulations), whereas there are no sissulations on the Many-Colored Tellin. **COLOR:** White to red (or may be rayed with white or red). **HABITAT:** Lives in high-salinity estuaries and offshore to depths of about 50 feet or more. Occasionally found on ocean beaches. **RANGE:** North Carolina to Florida and Texas. **NOTES:** Also called an Iris Tellin. **SCIENTIFIC NAME CHANGE:** Previous name: *Tellina iris* (Say, 1822). The species has been reassigned to the genus *Oudardia*.

....

Striate Tellin

Striate Tellin

Serratina aequistriata (Say, 1824)

DESCRIPTION: (1 inch) Oval, compressed shell. Beak back of center and higher than in most *Tellina* species (about three-quarters of total shell length). Surface covered with raised, thin concentric ribbing that is strongest toward the back end. Back edge a straight line but with distinctive radial ridges, two on the right valve and one on the left, making the back end appear bluntly pointed. Both lateral and cardinal teeth on hinge. Pallial sinus does not touch anterior muscle scar.

COLOR: White. HABITAT: Lives in mud flats south of Cape Hatteras, in high-salinity estuaries and offshore to depths of about 100 feet or more. Most common in offshore depths between 10 and 50 feet. Occasionally washed onto sound and ocean beaches. RANGE: North Carolina to Texas and Brazil. SCIENTIFIC NAME CHANGE: Previous name: *Tellina aequistriata* (Say, 1824). The species has been reassigned to the genus *Serratina*.

....

White Strigilla
Strigilla mirabilis (R. A. Philippi, 1841)

DESCRIPTION: (⅜ inch) Small, rounded, moderately inflated shell with off-center beak. Easily recognized by the strongly cut oblique lines on the surface. Large pallial sinus but difficult to see. Inner edge not crenulated. COLOR: Shiny white. HABITAT: Known to live offshore at depths of 10 feet to more than 100 feet off Beaufort Inlet and south. Occasionally washed onto ocean beaches south of Cape Hatteras. RANGE: North Carolina to Texas and Brazil. NOTES: Also called Remarkable Scraper.

White Strigilla

....

White-Crest Tellin
Tellidora cristata (Récluz, 1842) ·

DESCRIPTION: (1½ inch) Roughly ovate. Left valve very flat; the other only slightly inflated. Fine concentric ridges and dorsal margins with large, sawtooth crenulations in front and behind centrally placed beaks. COLOR: White. HABITAT: In sand in shallow nearshore water and in high-salinity estuaries. RANGE: Cape Hatteras to Yucatán, Mexico. NOTES: Single valves uncommon on beaches; found in Back Sound near Beaufort Inlet at 4-foot depth.

White-Crest Tellin

Speckled Tellin
Tellinella listeri (Röding, 1798)

DESCRIPTION: (3½ inch) Elongate, with a distinct posterior twist and two radial ridges at the posterior margin of the right valve. Numerous fine concentric threads. **COLOR:** Whitish with occasional zigzag specklings of purplish brown. Interior yellowish. **HABITAT:** Lives offshore to shelf edge; shells rarely wash ashore on beach. **RANGE:** Cape Hatteras to Brazil. **NOTES:** Commonly brought in with **Atlantic Calico Scallop** trawl fishery.

Speckled Tellin

DONACIDAE (WEDGECLAMS, COQUINAS)

Wedge shaped; colorful; common in ocean beach intertidal zone.

Fossor Coquina
Donax fossor (Say, 1822)

DESCRIPTION: (½ inch) Resembles the **Variable Coquina** except slightly elliptical and less triangular, with a smoother and more rounded posterior end. **COLOR:** Extremely variable coloration—white, yellow, orange, pink, red, and purple in solids or ringed or rayed patterns. **HABITAT:** Near and just below the low-tide line of ocean inlet beaches (lower on the beach than the Variable Coquina). **RANGE:** New York to Florida. **NOTES:** Populations of this species are known at the mouth of the Newport River at Fort Macon State Park. It should also be found at similar inlet locations farther south. **SCIENTIFIC NAME CHANGE:** *Donax parvulus* (R. A. Philippi, 1849) and *Donax fossor* (Say, 1822)

Fossor Coquina

have been found to be biologically and morphologically indistinguishable. *Donax fossor*, being the older name, has priority.

. . . .

Variable Coquina

Variable Coquina

Donax variabilis (Say, 1822)

DESCRIPTION: (1 inch) Small, elongate, triangular shell. Smooth exterior with ribbing at beak end of shell. Hinge teeth. COLOR: Extremely variable coloration—white, yellow, orange, pink, red, and purple in solids or ringed or rayed patterns. HABITAT: Lives in the intertidal zone of sandy ocean beaches. RANGE: New York to Texas. NOTES: Also called a Florida Coquina, Butterfly Shell, Wedge Shell, or Pompano. These clams actively migrate up and down the beach on each tidal cycle. Often seen along the tide line of sandy beaches, where waves continually uncover these shallowly buried clams and wash them farther up (or down) the beach. Each time the coquina is exposed, its small, muscular foot immediately emerges and stands the animal on end as it burrows down an inch or two into the wet sand. Coquinas can survive in dry sand for up to three days. See plate 11.

. . . .

SEMELIDAE (SEMELE CLAMS)

Roundish to oval-shaped shells; thin-shelled, mostly smooth; small spoon-shaped cavity in hinge; round pallial sinus.

Atlantic Abra

Abra aequalis (Say, 1822)

DESCRIPTION: (½ inch) Smooth, plump, almost circular shell. Beak area somewhat angular. Fine concentric ribbing near the edge of shell. Anterior edge of shell grooved. Thin-shelled. Hinge teeth. Large, rounded pallial sinus. Groove in right valve. **COLOR:** Exterior white and slightly iridescent. Whitish interior. **HABITAT:** Lives commonly in sounds, mouths of estuaries, and shallow offshore waters. Common on sound and ocean beaches. **RANGE:** Cape Hatteras to Brazil. **NOTES:** See **Cancellate Semele** notes.

Atlantic Abra

Smooth Abra

Abra lioica (Dall, 1881)

DESCRIPTION: (⅜ inch) Similar to the **Atlantic Abra** except shape more elongate, beak more forward and pronounced, and anterior edge of right valve not grooved. **COLOR:** Exterior white and slightly iridescent. Whitish interior. **HABITAT:** Lives in high-salinity estuaries and offshore to depths of about 100 feet. Occasionally found on ocean beaches. **RANGE:** Cape Cod, Massachusetts, to Florida and the Caribbean.

Smooth Abra

Tellin Semele

Cumingia sinuosa (A. Adams, 1850)

DESCRIPTION: (1 inch) Small, thin, oval shell with one end rounded and the other almost pointed. Many fine concentric ridges. Central beak. Spoon-shaped cavity in hinge area. Rounded pallial sinus. **COLOR:** White exterior and interior. **HABITAT:** Lives in sounds and shallow offshore water attached

Tellin Semele

to driftwood and shells. Occasionally found on ocean beaches. **RANGE:** Nova Scotia, Canada, to Florida. **NOTES:** Also called a Common Cumingia. See **Cancellate Semele** notes. **SCIENTIFIC NAME CHANGE:** The name *Cumingia tellinoides* (Conrad, 1831) is not available. It is replaced by the next available name, *Cumingia sinuosa* (A. Adams, 1850).

....

Concentric Ervilia
Ervilia concentrica (Holmes, 1860)

DESCRIPTION: (¼ inch) Oval shell with a slightly off-center beak. Many fine concentric ridges on surface. Triangular ligament pit on hinge and a prominent cardinal tooth on both valves. Large pallial sinus. **COLOR:** Cream exterior. Shiny and translucent interior. **HABITAT:** Lives offshore at 30-to-100-foot depths. Also has been found in the estuarine waters of Bogue Sound. Occasionally to commonly washed onto ocean beaches. **RANGE:** Cape Hatteras to Florida and Brazil.

Concentric Ervilia

....

Cancellate Semele
Semele bellastriata (Conrad, 1837)

DESCRIPTION: (1 inch) Small, oval, narrow shell. Radial and concentric ribbing on exterior, creating a very distinctive beaded look. Beak subcentral. Hinge teeth. Ligament embedded in spoon-shaped cavity in hinge area. Pallial sinus deep and rounded. Narrow lunule. **COLOR:** Cream exterior with pinkish-purple specks or blotches. Occasionally solid purplish gray. Shiny interior, often bright yellow or lavender. **HABITAT:** Lives offshore in sand and mud and has long siphons. Known at depths up to 300 feet. Occasionally found on ocean

Cancellate Semele

beaches south of Cape Hatteras. RANGE: Cape Hatteras to Florida, Texas, and Brazil. NOTES: This species tastes good but isn't abundant enough to be commercially valuable.

....

Atlantic Semele
Semele proficua (Pulteney, 1799)

DESCRIPTION: (1½ inches) Broadly oval to almost round shell. Fine, sharp concentric lines ¹⁄₁₆ inch apart. Central beak points forward. Small lunule. Lateral teeth on hinge and a narrow spoon-shaped cavity. Pallial sinus deep and rounded. COLOR: Creamy white exterior, sometimes with pinkish-red rays. Shiny white interior, sometimes yellowish with light reddish speckles. HABITAT: Lives in sounds and shallow offshore waters. Sometimes washed onto sound and ocean beaches. RANGE: Cape Hatteras to Argentina. NOTES: Also called a White Atlantic Semele. See **Cancellate Semele** notes.

Atlantic Semele

....

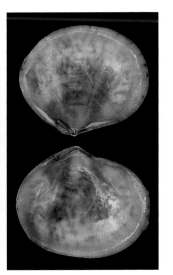

Purplish Semele
Semele purpurascens (Gmelin, 1791)

DESCRIPTION: (1¼ inch) Oblong. Thin-shelled. Very fine concentric growth threads over which run another set of fine, microscopic concentric lines at an oblique angle. COLOR: Gray or cream with purple or orangish mottling. Interior glossy. Central area suffused with more intense purple, brownish, or orange color. HABITAT: Lives offshore, in sand. RANGE: Cape Hatteras to Florida, the Caribbean, and Brazil. NOTES: Found in the **Atlantic Calico Scallop** fishery; occasionally washes ashore on beach.

Purplish Semele

SOLECURTIDAE (STOUT RAZOR CLAMS)

Long, compressed rectangular shells, top and ventral edges parallel; beak almost central. See also families Solenidae and Pharidae.

Corrugate Solecurtus

Corrugate Solecurtus
Solecurtus cumingianus (Dunker, 1862)

DESCRIPTION: (2¾ inches) Rectangular, gaping shell with bluntly rounded ends. Similar to **Stout Tagelus** except ends more rounded and the coarse concentric lines are overlain by sharp, oblique incised lines. Beak almost central. Small hinge teeth. COLOR: White exterior. Yellowish-gray periostracum. HABITAT: Lives offshore in sand or mud. Rarely found on ocean beaches. RANGE: North Carolina to Brazil. NOTES: Also called a Corrugated Razor Clam. It is able to burrow rapidly into sand.

Purplish Tagelus

Purplish Tagelus
Tagelus divisus (Spengler, 1794)

DESCRIPTION: (1¼ inches) Fragile, rectangular shell with rounded ends. Smooth surface with concentric growth lines not overlain by oblique lines. Beak almost central. Small hinge teeth. Distinctive purplish raised rib in interior running from the beak to the lower shell edge. Large pallial sinus. COLOR: Pale purplish-gray exterior, often with a faint reddish-brown streak near the edge. Purplish interior. Yellowish to greenish-brown periostracum. HABITAT: Lives in sounds and offshore. Commonly found washed onto sounds and ocean beaches. RANGE: Massachusetts to Brazil. NOTES:

It lives in vertical burrows and has long siphons that extend up to the surface. It is a suspension feeder.

. . . .

Stout Tagelus
Tagelus plebeius ([Lightfoot], 1786)

DESCRIPTION: (3½ inches) Strong, stout, rectangular shell resembling the **Corrugate Solecurtus**. Smooth surface with fine concentric lines not overlain by oblique lines. Beak almost central. Teeth on hinge. No vertical raised rib inside shell as in the **Purplish Tagelus**. Large pallial sinus. **COLOR:** Whitish exterior with no purplish rays. **HABITAT:** Lives in sounds. Commonly found washed onto sound and ocean beaches. **RANGE:** Massachusetts to Argentina. **NOTES:** See Purplish Tagelus notes.

Stout Tagelus

. . . .

UNGULINIDAE (DIPLODON CLAMS)

Small, round, inflated shells with two cardinal teeth (one is split).

. . . .

Atlantic Diplodon
Diplodonta punctata (Say, 1822)

DESCRIPTION: (½ inch or more) Strongly inflated, circular shell. Smooth surface incised with fine concentric growth lines. Thin-shelled. Two cardinal teeth on hinge of each valve, one of them split. No lateral teeth on hinge. **COLOR:** White. **HABITAT:** Lives offshore in sand at depths of 50 feet or more. Occasionally washed onto ocean beaches. **RANGE:** North Carolina to Florida and Brazil. **NOTES:** Note the drill hole made by a moonsnail in the photo.

Atlantic Diplodon

···

VENERIDAE (VENUS CLAMS)

Mostly roundish to oval shaped; beak points toward anterior; distinct impressed lunule in front of beak; prominent cardinal and lateral teeth; pallial sinus.

·········

False Quahog

Agriopoma morrhuanum (Dall, 1902)

DESCRIPTION: (1½ inches) Looks like a small quahog but not as heavy. Smooth concentric lines on exterior. Ventral edge not crenulated. Lateral and cardinal teeth on hinge. Lunule and pallial sinus. **COLOR:** Dull rusty-gray exterior. White interior. **HABITAT:** Offshore, mostly north of Cape Hatteras. Commonly found on ocean beaches. **RANGE:** Canada to North Carolina. **NOTES:** It is one of North Carolina's most common beach shells, but live specimens are rarely found. **SCIENTIFIC NAME CHANGE:** The name *Pitar morrhuanus* (Dall, 1902) was not properly established and cannot be accepted. The accepted name is *Agriopoma morrhuanum* (Dall 1902).

False Quahog

·········

Cross-Barred Venus

Chione elevata (Say, 1822)

DESCRIPTION: (1¾ inches) Rounded, triangular shell. Strong concentric ridges and strong radial ribbing form a raised crisscross pattern of ridges. Crenulations on ventral edge. Lateral and cardinal teeth on hinge. Lunule and small pallial sinus. **COLOR:** Grayish yellow–white exterior. Occasionally has a few lavender radial stripes. Interior usually purple. **HABITAT:** Commonly lives on muddy-sand bottoms of sounds and shallow

Cross-Barred Venus

offshore waters. Shells common on sound and ocean beaches. **RANGE:** North Carolina to Brazil. **NOTES:** Said to be sweeter tasting than the **Northern Quahog. SCIENTIFIC NAME CHANGE:** Recent study of this species has placed *Chione cancellata* (Linnaeus, 1767) in the southern Caribbean and *Chione elevata* (Say, 1822) in the northern Caribbean and Carolinian faunal provinces.

....

Gray Pygmy Venus

Gray Pygmy Venus
Chioneryx grus (Holmes, 1858)

DESCRIPTION: (⅜ inch) Oblong shell. Beak about one-quarter of the shell length from the rounded anterior end. Squarish back end. Surface with many fine radial ribs crossed by equally fine concentric lines. Lateral and cardinal teeth on hinge. Narrow, heart-shaped lunule. Small pallial sinus. **COLOR:** Exterior gray to white (sometimes light pink) with purplish brown near both ends of the hinge. Dark brown lunule. White interior with purplish brown near one end. **HABITAT:** Lives in sand and mud in high-salinity estuaries south of Cape Hatteras and in offshore waters up to 100 feet deep. Attaches to shells in shell-reef areas. Common on ocean beaches. **RANGE:** North Carolina to Florida and Texas. **SCIENTIFIC NAME CHANGE:** Previous name: *Chione grus* (Holmes, 1858). The species has been reassigned to genus *Chioneryx.*

Lady-in-Waiting Venus

·········

Lady-in-Waiting Venus
Chionopsis intapurpurea (Conrad, 1849)

DESCRIPTION: (1½ inches) Round, thick shell. Many concentric ridges closer set than those on the **Cross-Barred Venus**. Serrated lower edges of concentric ridges give appearance of being crossed by light ribbing. Lateral and cardinal teeth on hinge. Lunule and pallial sinus. Fine crenulations on ventral edge of shell. **COLOR:** Creamy white exterior, often with broken radial lavender stripes. White interior with purple markings. **HABITAT:** Lives offshore. Occasionally found on ocean beaches. **RANGE:** North Carolina to Brazil. **SCIENTIFIC NAME CHANGE:** Previous name: *Chione intapurpurea* (Conrad, 1849). The species has been reassigned to genus *Chionopsis*.

Atlantic Petricolid

·········

Atlantic Petricolid
Choristodon robustus (G. B. Sowerby I, 1834)

DESCRIPTION: (1 inch) Variable shape, usually oblong. Coarse radial ribs. Beak about one-quarter of length from anterior end. Deep pallial sinus. No good lateral teeth. **COLOR:** Grayish-white exterior and brownish interior. **HABITAT:** Lives offshore in nooks and crevices in and between rocks, shells, or coral. **RANGE:** North Carolina to Brazil. **NOTES:** Shell shape varies because it does not bore its own hole. Instead, it occupies crevices or holes bored by other animals and adopts the shape of the crevice or hole. **SCIENTIFIC NAME CHANGE:** The name *Rupellaria typica* (Jonas, 1844) is superseded by an earlier name, *Choristodon robustus* (G. B. Sowerby I, 1834).

Thin Cyclinella

Thin Cyclinella

Cyclinella tenuis (Récluz, 1852)

DESCRIPTION: (1¼ inches) Round, moderately inflated shell. Resembles a small *Dosinia* but lacks the closely spaced concentric ridges. Smooth surface with occasional concentric growth ridges. Small beak points forward noticeably. Thin-shelled. Faint lunule. Pallial sinus points toward beak. COLOR: Dull white exterior and interior. If present, periostracum is light gray. HABITAT: Lives in the soft bottoms of high-salinity estuaries and offshore. In North Carolina, collected mainly near Middle Marsh and at 30-foot depths off Atlantic Beach. RANGE: Virginia to Florida, Texas, and Brazil. NOTES: It is also called a Small Ring Clam and Atlantic Cyclinella.

Elegant Dosinia

Elegant Dosinia

Dosinia concentrica (Born, 1778)

DESCRIPTION: (4 inches) Round, flat, disklike shell. Similar to **Disk Dosinia** except for larger and less crowded concentric ridges—about 25 ridges per inch. Beak curves forward. Cardinal teeth on hinge. Lunule and pallial sinus. COLOR: Pure white exterior and interior. HABITAT: Lives offshore in deeper waters than those reported for the Disk Dosinia. Often found on Cape Lookout's ocean beaches. RANGE: North Carolina to Brazil. NOTES: Empty shells uncommonly found on beaches and rarely still attached at the hinge. SCIENTIFIC NAME CHANGE: The name *Dosinia elegans* (Conrad, 1843) is superseded by an earlier name, *Dosinia concentrica* (Born, 1778).

Disk Dosinia

Disk Dosinia
Dosinia discus (Reeve, 1850)

DESCRIPTION: (3 inches) Round, flat, disklike shell similar to **Elegant Dosinia**. Fine concentric ridges—about 50 ridges per inch. Beak curves forward. Cardinal teeth on hinge. Lunule and pallial sinus. COLOR: Shiny white interior and exterior. Thin, yellow periostracum. HABITAT: Lives in sounds and just offshore on shallow sand flats. Commonly found on sound and ocean beaches, often still attached at the hinge. RANGE: Virginia to Yucatán, Mexico.

Amethyst Gemclam

Amethyst Gemclam
Gemma gemma (Totten, 1834)

DESCRIPTION: (⅛ inch) Small, rounded, trigonal, and inflated. Exterior polished with numerous very fine concentric riblets. COLOR: Whitish to tan with purplish flush over the beaks and posterior. HABITAT: In muddy sand in high-salinity estuaries; in oyster beds in shallow water. RANGE: Nova Scotia, Canada, to Florida, Texas, and the Bahamas. NOTES: Very common but often overlooked because of small size. Introduced in Puget Sound, Washington.

Imperial Venus

Imperial Venus
Lirophora varicosa (G. B. Sowerby II, 1853)

DESCRIPTION: (1½ inches) Rounded, triangular, and well-inflated shell. Large, heavy concentric ridges rounded and often sharply shelved at the top. Ridges fragile on dry specimens. Bottom edge of ridges not serrated. Ventral edge of shell finely grooved. Cardinal and lateral teeth on hinge. Lunule and pallial sinus. COLOR: Tan exterior with lavender blotches and radial stripes. HABITAT: Lives offshore, south of Cape Hatteras, in 60-to-120-foot depths. Occasionally found on ocean beaches. RANGE: North Carolina to Brazil. NOTES: This species was frequently found among catches of the **Atlantic Calico Scallop** fishery. SCIENTIFIC NAME CHANGE: Previous name, *Chione latilirata* (Conrad, 1841), refers to a fossil only. The accepted name for the living species is *Lirophora varicosa* (G. B. Sowerby II, 1853).

Sunray Venus
Macrocallista nimbosa ([Lightfoot], 1786)

DESCRIPTION: (7½ inches) Large, smooth, glassy, elongate to triangular shell with rounded ends. Light concentric and radial lines. Lateral and cardinal teeth on hinge. Large lunule and small pallial sinus. No crenulations on ventral margin. COLOR: Grayish-salmon exterior, often with dull lavender radial stripes (colors fade rapidly in the sun). Glossy whitish interior. HABITAT: Lives from intertidal zone of sounds to offshore depths greater than 65 feet. It buries itself just below the surface. Commonly found on sound and ocean beaches below Cape Hatteras (particularly Cape Lookout). RANGE: North Carolina to Texas. NOTES:

Sunray Venus

Of interest for potential aquaculture in North
Carolina in the 2020s, this clam makes an excellent chowder. See plate 12.

....

Calico Clam

Calico Clam
Megapitaria maculata (Linnaeus, 1758)

DESCRIPTION: (3½ inches) Round to oval-shaped
shell with smooth, shiny surface. Lateral and
cardinal teeth on hinge. Lunule and large pallial
sinus. Ventral margin not crenulated. **COLOR:**
Creamy exterior with purplish-brown checkerboard pattern and usually one or two darker
radiating bands. Polished white interior. **HABITAT:**
Lives offshore at 50-to-120-foot depths south
of Cape Lookout. The animal buries itself in
the sand. Occasionally found on ocean beaches
south of Cape Hatteras. **RANGE:** North Carolina
to Brazil. **NOTES:** Also called a Checkerboard
Clam or Spotted Venus. Many say this species
tastes delicious. See plate 13. **SCIENTIFIC NAME
CHANGE:** Previous name: *Macrocallista maculata*
(Linnaeus, 1758). The species has been reassigned
to genus *Megapitaria*.

....

Southern Quahog

Southern Quahog
Mercenaria campechiensis (Gmelin 1791)

DESCRIPTION: (6 inches) Heavy, rounded, inflated
shell. Closely related to the **Northern Quahog**
except surface sharply ridged in the central area.
Many concentric ridges on surface. Strong lateral
and cardinal teeth on hinge. Lunule and pallial
sinus. Fine crenulations on ventral margin. **COLOR:**
Dull grayish-white exterior. Interior usually all
white but occasionally tinged with some purple.
HABITAT: Lives offshore in fine sand near inlets at

depths of 40 to 50 feet or more. Commonly found washed onto ocean beaches. RANGE: Virginia to Texas. NOTES: A bed between Cape Lookout and Beaufort Inlet was fished commercially at one time. The Northern and Southern Quahogs seem to hybridize near North Carolina inlets. Hybrid specimens may grow to 6 inches long.

....

Northern Quahog
Mercenaria mercenaria (Linnaeus, 1758)

Northern Quahog

DESCRIPTION: (4½ inches) Heavy, rounded, somewhat inflated shell. Concentric ridges on surface smooth near the center and stronger near the lower edge. Elevated beak. Strong lateral and cardinal teeth on hinge, well-defined lunule, deep pallial sinus. COLOR: Dull gray exterior, occasionally with purple zigzag markings. Dull gray interior, often with some dark purple near the pallial sinus. HABITAT: Lives in sounds and mouths of estuaries near the ocean. Commonly found on sound and ocean beaches. RANGE: Canada to Texas. NOTES: Also known as the Hard-Shelled Clam, Littleneck Clam, Cherry Stone, and Chowder Clam. A large commercial fishery in North Carolina waters, it has potential for mariculture. Nearly all individuals are male the first year; then about half become females. It was a favorite food of early Native Americans, who made beads from these shells' purple edges and used them as wampum (money). A form of this species with purple zigzag markings was once given the subspecies name *Mercenaria mercenaria notata* (Say, 1822), but this clam is a naturally occurring genetic color form of the Northern Quahog. The purple zigzag pattern occurs in a number of other species in the family Veneridae. Specimens with these markings were once specifically bred by clam growers to distinguish their stock from non-hatchery-bred clams. Clams with these markings may still occasionally be found.

False Angelwing

False Angelwing

Petricolaria pholadiformis (Lamarck, 1818)

DESCRIPTION: (2¾ inches) Thin, elongate shell resembling a small **Angelwing** but lacks the rolled-out hinge area. Beak at one end of shell. Strong radial ribbing on the beak end. Teeth on hinge. Deep pallial sinus. COLOR: White exterior and interior. HABITAT: Lives in intertidal zone, burrowed into hard clay or peat. Commonly found on sounds and ocean beaches. RANGE: Canada to Uruguay. NOTES: It burrows into hard surfaces and has long, partially united siphons. As suggested by the species name, it could easily be confused with the Angelwing family Pholadidae. SCIENTIFIC NAME CHANGE: Previous name: *Petricola pholadiformis* (Lamarck, 1818). The species has been reassigned to the genus *Petricolaria*.

MYIDAE (SOFTSHELL CLAMS)

Thin elliptical shell; hinge has horizontal spoon-shaped shelf extending from hinge plate in left valve.

Softshell Clam

Softshell Clam

Mya arenaria (Linnaeus, 1758)

DESCRIPTION: (3½ inches) Elliptical shell with fine concentric lines. Left valve has spoon-shaped depression on a horizontal shelf that projects from the hinge area. Beak near center. Deep pallial sinus. COLOR: White to gray exterior. White interior. Grayish-brown periostracum. HABITAT: Lives in sounds and inlets with small specimens found south of Cape Hatteras. Large fossil shells frequently found on ocean beaches. Lives buried in mud and has long siphons. Adaptations allow it to survive exposure to air twice a day in the intertidal zone. RANGE: Arctic Ocean to Labrador, Canada, and Cape Hatteras (formerly to South Carolina). Winter currents carry larvae southward into Pamlico Sound, where juvenile clams (12 to 15 mm) grow annually but do not survive the spring and summer water temperatures there. NOTES: Also known as the Steamer Clam, it is a major fishery in some northern states. Its delicious meat is the source for many fried clams.

CORBULIDAE (CORBULA CLAMS)

Small, chunky, oval shells; right valve larger, thicker, and overlapping the left; right valve with single strong cardinal tooth fitting into notch in left valve. Corbulas are difficult to identify because of their variable shapes; at least three more species (*Caryocorbula nasuta* [G. B. Sowerby I, 1833], *Caryocorbula swiftiana* [C. B. Adams, 1852], and *Corbula operculata* [R. A. Philippi, 1848]) are found regularly in North Carolina waters.

Contracted Corbula

Rose Corbula

....

Contracted Corbula
Caryocorbula contracta (Say, 1822)

DESCRIPTION: (⅜ inch) Small, chunky, oval shell with angular ridge running down its back side. Central beak. Surface covered with many slightly irregular, raised concentric lines. Triangular tooth on right valve projects outward just below the beak. V-shaped notch on left valve just in front of the beak. COLOR: Gray exterior. Whitish interior. HABITAT: Lives offshore in sand or mud at depths up to 100 feet. Occasionally lives in high-salinity estuaries. Commonly found on ocean beaches. RANGE: Cape Cod, Massachusetts, to Florida and Brazil. NOTES: This species is often found in the stomach of the sea star *Astropecten articulatus*. Corbulas are difficult to identify because of their variable shapes. See the family Corbulidae notes. SCIENTIFIC NAME CHANGE: Previous name: *Corbula contracta* (Say, 1822). The species has been re-assigned to genus *Caryocorbula*.

....

Rose Corbula
Corbula dietziana (C. B. Adams, 1852)

DESCRIPTION: (½ inch) Similar to **Contracted Corbula** except with (1) heavier and thicker shell, (2) coarser concentric ridges with microscopic threads between them, and (3) very angular posterior ridge and posterior margin. COLOR: Gray to pinkish exterior. Pink rays often on ventral edges. HABITAT: Lives offshore in sand to depths of about 100 feet. Commonly on ocean beaches. RANGE: North Carolina to Florida and Brazil. NOTES: This species is occasionally found in the stomach of the sea star *Astropecten articulatus*. It has two growth phases. The first is that of a typical bivalve, with both valves growing at the same rate. In the second phase, the right valve grows nearly three times as much as the left valve. This change in growth produces part of the shell that is thicker and more angular than it was in the earlier phase. Common name changed from Dietz Corbula to Rose Corbula.

....

PHOLADIDAE (PIDDOCK CLAMS AND ANGELWINGS)

Bivalves adapted for burrowing or boring deeply into mud, clay, untreated wood, or soft rock. Generally ovate to cylindrical shells; complex hinge area with a rolled-back, or reflected, flange of shell covered in life by separate (loose) accessory plates; long, easily broken, spinelike (or spoonlike) projection (apophysis) in each valve; deep pallial sinus in the pallial line.

....

Atlantic Mud-Piddock

Atlantic Mud-Piddock
Barnea truncata (Say, 1822)

DESCRIPTION: (2¼ inches) Similar to **Angelwing** but with weaker sculpture. Anterior end squared off and posterior end pointed. Loose accessory plates above the hinge on live specimens. COLOR: White exterior and interior. HABITAT: Lives burrowed into mud, clay, or soft driftwood. Occasionally washed onto sounds and ocean beaches. RANGE: Maine to Brazil. NOTES: Also called a Fallen Angelwing. This fragile shell is rarely dug from mud without breaking. It burrows deeply and has long, united siphons.

Angelwing

Angelwing

Cyrtopleura costata (Linnaeus, 1758)

DESCRIPTION: (5¾ inches) Fairly large, elongate shell tapers to a posterior rounded point. The open paired shells strongly resemble a medieval artistic rendition of the wings of an angel. About 30 sharply beaded ribs. Shell rolls outward on top—this edge is not braced by partitions. Very thin shell breaks easily. COLOR: Pure white exterior and interior, occasionally pink at the edges. Grayish periostracum. HABITAT: Lives offshore and in estuaries, burrowed up to 3 feet deep in mud or clay. Occasionally washed onto beaches. RANGE: New Jersey to Brazil. NOTES: This is a popular shell with delicious meat. The pink tinges occur when the animal feeds on a certain type of algae. It moves up and down in its burrows. If dug up, the fragile shell must be placed immediately into a container of water or it will close suddenly and shatter. Small specimens could be confused with **False Angelwing**.

in situ

Spiny Piddock

Spiny Piddock

Jouannetia quillingi (R. D. Turner, 1955)

DESCRIPTION: (¾ inch) Thin, fragile. Valves divided by a sharply depressed oblique radial center line, with sculpture of thin concentric ridges meeting on the center line at a 90-degree angle. Ridges edged with tiny spines that protrude from posterior edge. COLOR: White. HABITAT: Submerged, waterlogged wood or soft rock. RANGE: North Carolina to Florida and Texas. NOTES: A common boring clam burrowing into offshore rock outcrops in "live bottom." Occasionally washes ashore, deeply buried in driftwood. Otherwise rarely seen.

Wedge Piddock

....

Wedge Piddock
Martesia cuneiformis (Say, 1822)

DESCRIPTION: (½ inch) Tiny, wedge-shaped shell with concentric ridges. Exterior groove runs from beak to ventral edge of each valve. Hinge line topped with a series of loose accessory plates. COLOR: Whitish exterior, usually with brown stains. Whitish interior. HABITAT: Lives burrowed in submerged driftwood. RANGE: North Carolina to Brazil. NOTES: Also called a Wedge-Shaped Martesia. It is one of about six small boring clams found in North Carolina waters. Species are distinguished mainly by characteristics of their accessory plates. It destroys many wooden structures along the coast.

Campeche Angelwing

....

Campeche Angelwing
Pholas campechiensis (Gmelin, 1791)

DESCRIPTION: (3¾ inches) Resembles the **Angelwing** but is smaller and less inflated at the anterior end, with weaker ribbing and numerous braces supporting the rolled-back hinge on its top surface. COLOR: White exterior and interior. HABITAT: Lives offshore, burrowed deeply in stiff mud. Occasionally washed onto ocean beaches near and south of Cape Fear. RANGE: North Carolina to Uruguay. NOTES: Live specimens rarely are found. Small specimens could be confused with **False Angelwing**.

....

HIATELLIDAE (HIATELLA CLAMS AND GEODUCKS)

There are only two, very different, species in North Carolina: one a quite large, deeply burrowing clam in offshore and high-salinity waters; the other a common denizen of nooks, crannies, and crevices in rocks, shells, and offshore wrecks.

....

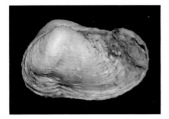

Arctic Hiatella

Arctic Hiatella

Hiatella arctica (Linnaeus, 1767)

DESCRIPTION: (1 inch) The shell is often irregularly shaped because of its "nestling" and burrowing habits but is generally elongate with parallel margins. Somewhat rectangular, with a conspicuous external ligament. Irregular growth lines. Radial rib at the posterior end. Gray, thin periostracum. COLOR: Chalky white. HABITAT: Attaches in crevices and to vegetation with holdfasts from near shore to deep water. RANGE: Widely distributed from the Arctic to Brazil. NOTES: Common offshore on and among rocks and other hard substrates. Frequently washed ashore on beaches. Extremely variable shell morphology within this genus.

....

Atlantic Geoduck

Atlantic Geoduck

Panopea bitruncata (Conrad, 1872)

DESCRIPTION: (8¼ inches) Large, nearly rectangular shell with a broadly rounded anterior end and a blunt, slightly concave posterior end. Rough concentric ridges on surface but smooth ventral edge. Teeth on hinge. Short but indented pallial sinus. COLOR: White to cream exterior and interior. **HABITAT:** Lives in shallow to offshore waters in burrows up to 4 feet deep. A bed of empty shells is known off Atlantic Beach near an artificial reef of sunken ships. Occasionally found on ocean beaches. **RANGE:** North Carolina to Texas. **NOTES:** The closely related Pacific Geoduck from Puget Sound is reportedly one of the finest-tasting clams found along the West Coast and is intensively cultured commercially. Its previous scientific name, *Panopea abrupta* (Conrad, 1849), now applies to a fossil only. The accepted name for the recent Pacific species is *Panopea generosa* (A. Gould, 1850).

....

SOLENIDAE (JACKKNIFE CLAMS)

Long, narrow shell; dorsal edge straight; ventral edge curved; beak at anterior end. Animals burrow deeply into sandy mud; called *couteau* (knife) in France. See also family Solecurtidae.

....

Green Jackknife

Green Jackknife
Solen viridis (Say, 1821)

DESCRIPTION: (1½ inches) Long, slender shell similar to the **Atlantic Jackknife** but shorter and less curved. Four to five times as long as high. Hinge line almost straight but possibly slightly curved. One cardinal tooth in hinge of each valve. **COLOR:** Grayish-white exterior and interior. Yellowish-green periostracum. **HABITAT:** Lives in sounds and intertidal sandbars. Occasionally washed onto sound and ocean beaches in shell drift at tide line. **RANGE:** Rhode Island to Texas. **NOTES:** See Atlantic Jackknife notes.

....

PHARIDAE (RAZOR CLAMS, JACKKNIFE CLAMS)

Long, narrow shell; top and ventral edges parallel; beak at anterior end. Animals burrow deeply into sandy mud; called *couteau* (knife) in France. See also family Solecurtidae.

....

Atlantic Jackknife

Atlantic Jackknife
Ensis leei (M. Huber, 2015)

DESCRIPTION: (5 inches) Long, slender shell six times as long as high. Slightly curved with blunt ends. Looks like an old-fashioned straight razor. Cardinal and lateral hinge teeth behind the beak. COLOR: Whitish exterior. White and violet interior. Shiny olive to brown periostracum. HABITAT: Lives in sounds and offshore burrowing in muddy sand. Common on ocean beaches, particularly north of Cape Hatteras. Often found in shell drift at tide line. RANGE: Canada to South Carolina. NOTES: This species is excellent tasting but not fished commercially. It burrows rapidly into sand and swims in an erratic manner. Edges of the shell are sharp. See **Minor Jackknife** notes. SCIENTIFIC NAME CHANGE: Previous name, *Ensis directus* (Conrad, 1844), applies to a fossil only. The newly accepted name for the recent species is *Ensis leei* (M. Huber, 2015).

....

Minor Jackknife

Minor Jackknife
Ensis minor (Chenu, 1843)

DESCRIPTION: (5 inches, but most are about 1¾ inches) Similar to the **Atlantic Jackknife** except smaller, more fragile, and possibly more pointed at the toothless end of the hinge. About nine times as long as high. COLOR: Whitish exterior. Interior stained with purple. Reportedly paler than the Atlantic Jackknife. HABITAT: Lives offshore burrowed in muddy sand at depths to about 60 feet and in moderate-to-high-salinity estuaries. Commonly washed onto ocean beaches. RANGE: New Jersey to Texas. NOTES: Also called a Dwarf Razor Clam or Common Razor Clam. It is often eaten by wading birds. Some authorities formerly questioned whether this might be a subspecies of the Atlantic Jackknife. Most small specimens found south of the Cape Lookout area will most likely be the Minor Jackknife. SCIENTIFIC NAME CHANGE: Previously known as *Ensis minor* (Dall, 1899). The current valid name is *Ensis minor* (Chenu, 1843).

....

GASTROCHAENIDAE (CHIMNEY CLAMS, FLASK CLAMS)

Narrow, fan shape; beak near anterior end; wide gape along most of lower edge; extremely long, nonretractable siphons in life.

....

Atlantic Gastrochaenid

Atlantic Gastrochaenid
Lamychaena hians (Gmelin, 1791)

DESCRIPTION: (⅝ inch) Elliptical shell. Resembles a mussel or piddock with beak close to the anterior end. Large gape just behind beak. Thin-shelled. Small hinge teeth. COLOR: Chalky white exterior. White interior. HABITAT: Lives offshore, burrowed inside hard corals, limestone, and large, heavy shells (e.g., *Mercenaria*), in association with other rock borers (*Lithophaga*, *Jouannetia*) and crevice dwellers (*Hiatella*). Occasionally lives in high-salinity estuarine areas such as Wreck Point and Cape Lookout. Collected by scuba divers at a 70-foot depth off Wrightsville Beach (burrowed into rock). **RANGE:** North Carolina to Brazil. **NOTES:** Common name changed from Atlantic Rocellaria to Atlantic Gastrochaenid. Also called an Atlantic Gastrochaena. This species excavates flask-shaped burrows in coral rock that are flask-like and lined with a calcareous substance. It has long siphons. A related species, *Gastrochaena ovata* (G. B. Sowerby I, 1834), also occurs in North Carolina. **SCIENTIFIC NAME CHANGE:** Previous name: *Gastrochaena hians* (Gmelin, 1791). The species has been reassigned to genus *Lamychaena.*

PANDORIDAE (PANDORA CLAMS)

Small, crescent shaped; slightly inflated convex left valve and fairly flat right valve; pearly interior; no pallial sinus; strong cardinal teeth.

Threeline Pandora

Threeline Pandora
Pandora trilineata (Say, 1822)

DESCRIPTION: (1 inch) Small, crescent-shaped, flat shell with one end shaped like a small tube. Concave upper edge. Rough concentric growth lines on surface. Strong cardinal teeth radiating from beak. Worn shells with pearly layer below. No pallial sinus. **COLOR:** White exterior. Pearly interior. **HABITAT:** Lives buried just below the surface in sounds and shallow offshore areas. Rarely seen on beaches by collectors. **RANGE:** Virginia to Texas. **NOTES:** Also called Say's Pandora. Four more related species of pandora clams are found in North Carolina in this habitat. One is restricted to north of Cape Hatteras and the other three occur south of Cape Hatteras, generally farther offshore than *Pandora trilineata*. They have short, united siphons.

....

LYONSIIDAE (LYONSIA CLAMS)

Thin, pearly shell; left valve more convex and larger, overlapping the right valve; no hinge teeth; sometimes nestles into tight spaces and becomes misshapen as a result.

....

Glassy Lyonsia

Glassy Lyonsia
Lyonsia hyalina (Conrad, 1831)

DESCRIPTION: (¾ inch) Small, very fragile shell with rounded ends. Beak not central but located about one-third of the way in from shell's posterior end. Fine radial ribbing on surface. No teeth on hinge. Sand grains often stuck to the periostracum. COLOR: Pearly grayish-white exterior. White interior. Yellowish-brown periostracum. HABITAT: Lives in high-salinity estuaries and offshore. RANGE: Canada to South Carolina. NOTES: A closely related species, the Pearly Entodesma or Pearly Lyonsia (*Entodesma brasiliense* [A. Gould, 1850]), is occasionally found offshore in sponges. Generally larger and more swollen at its anterior end than the Glassy Lyonsia, it has been noted by scuba divers in the Cape Fear area.

PERIPLOMATIDAE (SPOONCLAMS)

Thin pearly shell; right valve usually more convex and overlapping left valve near the beak; internal ligament is accommodated within a spoonlike extension and groove near the beak in both valves; no hinge teeth; pallial sinus.

Oval Spoonclam

Oval Spoonclam
Cochlodesma leanum (Conrad, 1831)

DESCRIPTION: (1¾ inches) Oval shell with one end slightly squared off. Left valve less convex than right valve. Spoon-shaped cavity in hinge area of both valves, beginning as a narrow slit in the beak and extending into the shell cavity. Blunt anterior end of shell has internal rib or crease running from hinge cavity to about halfway down the lower edge. Fine, raised rib running parallel to crease reinforces the spoon-shaped cavity. No cardinal or lateral teeth on hinge. Small pallial sinus. **COLOR:** White exterior and interior. Yellow periostracum. **HABITAT:** Lives just offshore, mostly north of Cape Hatteras. Not commonly washed onto ocean beaches. **RANGE:** Nova Scotia, Canada, to North Carolina. **NOTES:** Common name changed from Lea Spoonclam to Oval Spoonclam. **SCIENTIFIC NAME CHANGE:** Previous name: *Periploma leanum* (Conrad, 1831). The species has been reassigned to genus *Cochlodesma*.

Species
Descriptions
Gastropods

....

THE FOLLOWING LIST OF FAMILIES within the class Gastropoda found in North Carolina are arranged in taxonomic and phylogenetic order based on the new classification of Gastropoda (Bouchet et al., 2017). In the species descriptions, shapes are often general due to the wide character variability within most molluscan families. See also the illustrations of general shell shapes for gastropods in the "How to Use This Guide" section. In some species descriptions, a width is provided when that measurement is more critical than the length.

Fissurellidae	Ficidae	Columbellidae	Bullidae
Calliostomatidae	Strombidae	Fasciolariidae	Tornatinidae
Turbinidae	Tonnidae	Nassariidae	Pyramidellidae
Cerithiidae	Bursidae	Pisaniidae	Ellobiidae
Turritellidae	Cassidae	Muricidae	
Epitoniidae	Charoniidae	Costellariidae	
Littorinidae	Cymatiidae	Olividae	
Naticidae	Personidae	Conidae	
Cerithiopsidae	Xenophoridae	Clathurellidae	
Eulimidae	Marginellidae	Drilliidae	
Calyptraeidae	Volutidae	Mangeliidae	
Cypraeidae	Cancellariidae	Pseudomelatomidae	
Ovulidae	Busyconidae*	Terebridae	
Triviidae	Colidae*	Architectonicidae	

*In the 2017 reclassification of gastropods, the whelks (Busyconidae) and colus (Colidae) were shown as subfamilies within Buccinidae. However, this was still being studied in 2023; thus, for this revision of *Seashells of North Carolina*, these species will continue to be shown as the families Busyconidae and Colidae.

Gastropods by Family

FISSURELLIDAE (KEYHOLE LIMPETS)

Low, cone-like shell shape, with a "keyhole" near the apex; water is drawn under the edge of the shell and across the gills and passed out through the keyhole; shell width can be greater than shell height.

Cayenne Keyhole Limpet

Cayenne Keyhole Limpet
Diodora cayenensis (Lamarck, 1822)

DESCRIPTION: (1 inch) Shell shaped like a small, low cone. Many ribs radiate from a small, sub-central keyhole-like opening on top of shell. Inside of keyhole, opening outlined by a truncate callus with a deep pit on its concave edge. COLOR: Exterior white and pinkish gray or brown. Interior white to gray. HABITAT: Lives in inlets and offshore waters attached to rocks or shells. Occasionally found on sound and ocean beaches. RANGE: New Jersey to Brazil. NOTES: Also called a Little Keyhole Limpet. An herbivore, it uses a radula to scrape algae off rocks. Its powerful foot creates strong suction to keep waves from washing it off the rocks. A very similar species, *Diodora sayi* (Dall, 1889), lives on offshore reef structures south of Cape Lookout but is unlikely to wash ashore.

CALLIOSTOMATIDAE (TOPSNAILS)

Shell resembles a toy top with beaded spiral cords; interior not iridescent; shell width can be greater than shell height; umbilicus may be open or closed (absent).

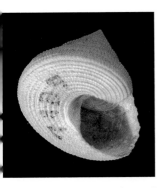

Sculptured Topsnail

Sculptured Topsnail

Calliostoma euglyptum (A. Adams, 1855)

DESCRIPTION: (1 inch wide) Similar in shape to the **Beautiful Topsnail** but larger, with beaded spiral ridges of equal strength (not stronger near whorl sutures). Rounded body whorl. Round or elliptical aperture. Operculum. No umbilicus. **COLOR:** Yellow-brown or pinkish exterior, sometimes with dark brown bars running the width of the whorl. Iridescent interior. **HABITAT:** Lives on offshore reefs and wrecks, and on rock jetties near inlets. Rarely found on ocean beaches. **RANGE:** North Carolina to Texas. **NOTES:** See Beautiful Topsnail notes.

Beautiful Topsnail

Beautiful Topsnail

Calliostoma pulchrum (C. B. Adams, 1850)

DESCRIPTION: (½ inch wide) Tiny shell shaped like a top or cone with flat sides. Length and width of shell nearly equal. Surface not rough but has finely beaded spiral ridges, stronger near the whorl sutures. No umbilicus. Round or elliptical aperture. Operculum. **COLOR:** Yellow-brown exterior with reddish spots. Iridescent interior. **HABITAT:** Lives in sounds and just offshore. Occasionally found on sound and ocean beaches. **RANGE:** North Carolina to Florida. **NOTES:** Also called a Beautiful Top Shell. This species is an herbivore. Young are free-swimming. Topsnails are difficult to identify. Most are found in areas not readily accessible to the average collector.

Depressed Topsnail

....

Depressed Topsnail

Calliostoma yucatecanum (Dall, 1881)

DESCRIPTION: (½ inch wide) Small shell shaped like a top with flat sides. Many spiral cords. Rounded body whorl. Broader than the **Sculptured Topsnail**, with a deep umbilicus. Round or elliptical aperture. Operculum. **COLOR:** Yellow to pink exterior with dark spots or bars. Iridescent interior. **HABITAT:** Lives offshore. Common as bycatch in the **Atlantic Calico Scallop** fishery. **RANGE:** North Carolina to Yucatán, Mexico. **NOTES:** Also called a Yucatan Top Shell. See **Beautiful Topsnail** notes.

TURBINIDAE (TURBANS, STARSNAILS)

Resemble a turban; interior iridescent; shell width can be greater than shell height.

Longspine Starsnail

....

Longspine Starsnail

Lithopoma phoebium (Röding, 1798)

DESCRIPTION: (2 inches wide, including spines) Heavy, top-shaped shell with triangular spines radiating from flat whorls, resembling the sun. Flat base of shell about twice as wide as tall. Beaded spiral cords. Low or slightly raised spire. Thick, oval, calcareous operculum. **COLOR:** Cream to tan exterior. Iridescent silver interior. **HABITAT:** Offshore on rocky or shelly bottoms and shipwrecks. Collected by scuba divers at depths greater than 60 feet. **RANGE:** Cape Hatteras to Florida and Brazil. **NOTES:** Also called a Longspine Star Shell. Females release eggs into the water. Young are free-swimming. **SCIENTIFIC NAME**

CHANGE: Previous name: *Astralium phoebium* (Röding, 1798). The species has been reassigned to the genus *Lithopoma*.

Chestnut Turban

Chestnut Turban

Turbo castanea (Gmelin, 1791)

DESCRIPTION: (1½ inches) Heavy, top-shaped shell resembling a turban. Rounded whorls. Outer surface rough, knobby, and beaded. Rounded or elliptical aperture. Round, calcareous operculum. COLOR: Exterior gray, brown, or greenish with brown splotches. Interior iridescent and shiny. White operculum. HABITAT: Lives near inlets and offshore. Occasionally washed onto ocean beaches. RANGE: North Carolina to Brazil. NOTES: Also called a Knobby Turban. This species is an herbivore. Females release eggs into the water. Young are free-swimming. It is related to a Pacific shell called a Cat's-eye.

CERITHIIDAE (CERITHS, BITTIUMS)

Slender shell with high, pointed spires; small, near-circular aperture with distinct siphonal canal.

Grass Cerith

Grass Cerith

Bittiolum varium (L. Pfeiffer, 1840)

DESCRIPTION: (¼ inch) Very small shell. A long, slender spire. Network pattern on surface created by spiral lines crossing vertical ribs. Usually one thickened rib on body whorl. COLOR: Grayish-brown and white exterior. HABITAT: Lives in high-salinity estuaries. RANGE: Canada to Brazil.

NOTES: Also called a Variable Bittium. This species is common in shallow eelgrass beds and may be seen crawling on hard substrates during early summer. It feeds on detritus and algae. SCIENTIFIC NAME CHANGE: Previous name: *Bittium varium* (L. Pfeiffer, 1840). The species has been reassigned to the genus *Bittiolum.*

....

Dark Cerith

Dark Cerith
Cerithium atratum (Born, 1778)

DESCRIPTION: (1¾ inches) Slender, high-spired, heavy-looking shell. Knobby, well-beaded spiral lines more prominent than axial ribs. Prominent siphonal canal at bottom of aperture. Small operculum. COLOR: Cream exterior stained with brownish gray. HABITAT: Lives in sounds and near inlets south of Cape Hatteras. Occasionally washed onto beaches. RANGE: North Carolina to Brazil. NOTES: Also called a Florida Cerith or Florida Horn Shell. This species feeds on detritus and algae on rocks or sand. Young are free-swimming.

TURRITELLIDAE (TURRETSNAILS, WORMSNAILS)

Two very distinctive shell forms: both slender shells with high, sharply pointed spire and sharply pointed, round-to-squarish aperture; in wormsnails, the later whorls may become loosely coiled and considered wormlike.

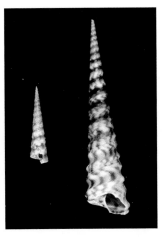

Eastern Turretsnail

Eastern Turretsnail

Turritella exoleta (Linnaeus, 1758)

DESCRIPTION: (2¾ inches) Small to medium, slender, tightly coiled shell with a high, sharply pointed spire. Strong, smooth spiral cord at top and bottom of each whorl and concave between. Round aperture with a thin lip. No siphonal canal. Bristles on edge of operculum. COLOR: Whitish exterior with brownish markings. HABITAT: Lives in deep offshore waters. RANGE: North Carolina to Brazil. NOTES: Also called a Common Turret Shell. This species is a filter feeder. See plate 14.

Florida Wormsnail

Florida Wormsnail

Vermicularia knorrii (Deshayes, 1843)

DESCRIPTION: (tight coil: ½ inch) Tightly coiled shell apex resembling miniature turretsnail. Later whorls are loose and coil without apparent direction. COLOR: Exterior whitish near tip and yellowish brown elsewhere. HABITAT: Lives offshore. Frequently colonial in sponge masses; sometimes in tangled clusters of multiple individuals. Occasionally washed onto ocean beaches. RANGE: North Carolina to Gulf of Mexico. NOTES: Also called Knorr's Worm Shell. Shells may become entangled with others and look like a large, multiple-worm mass. This species is a filter feeder.

EPITONIIDAE (WENTLETRAPS, JANTHINAS)

Two very distinctive groups, long considered separate families, were recently recognized as genera within a single family (Bouchet et al., 2017). The wentletraps have a high spire; round, circular aperture with no siphonal canal and no umbilicus; whorls rounded and sculptured with distinctive, bladelike axial ribs. The term "wentletrap" is derived from the Dutch word *wenteltrap*, denoting a spiral staircase. Epitoniidae now includes janthinas, the purple sea snails formerly in the family Janthinidae.

Reticulate Wentletrap

Reticulate Wentletrap
Amaea retifera (Dall, 1889)

DESCRIPTION: (1 inch) High, slender spire. Network pattern on surface created by many bladelike ribs that cross spiral ridges. Ridges weaker than ribs. Round aperture. Operculum. COLOR: Straw-yellow to pale brown exterior, some with dark spots. HABITAT: Lives offshore. Occurs in areas fished for **Atlantic Calico Scallops**. RANGE: North Carolina to Brazil. NOTES: See **Brown-Band Wentletrap** notes.

Angulate Wentletrap

Angulate Wentletrap
Epitonium angulatum (Say, 1831)

DESCRIPTION: (1 inch) High, slender, glossy spire. Each whorl with 9 to 10 strong ribs, each slightly angled on the whorl shoulder. Smooth spaces between ribs. Round aperture. Operculum. COLOR: Shiny white interior and exterior. Reddish-brown operculum. **HABITAT**: Common in drift on ocean beaches. Sometimes confused with **Humphrey's Wentletrap**. **RANGE**: New York to Uruguay. **NOTES**: See **Brown-Band Wentletrap** notes. See plate 15.

. . . .

Champion's Wentletrap

Champion's Wentletrap

Epitonium championi (Clench and R. D. Turner, 1952)

DESCRIPTION: (½ inch) Aperture subcircular 10 to 11 whorls; has 8 or 9 flattened costae. 19 to 20 incised spiral lines around whorls. Spire angle 20 degrees. **COLOR**: Flat white to light cream. **HABITAT**: Intertidal to depth of 120 feet; occasionally found on ocean beaches. **RANGE**: Massachusetts to northeast Florida. **NOTES**: Easily overlooked and mistaken for **Humphrey's Wentletrap**; the incised spiral lines can be near microscopic.

. . . .

Humphrey's Wentletrap

Humphrey's Wentletrap

Epitonium humphreysii (Kiener, 1838)

DESCRIPTION: (¾ inch) Small, high-spired shell. Very similar to **Angulate Wentletrap** in appearance, habitat, and number but has eight to nine rounded ribs on each whorl, thicker and not angulate at shoulder. Also, generally more slender, with a thicker lip on round aperture. Smooth spaces between ribs. Operculum. **COLOR**: White exterior and interior. Mahogany operculum. **HABITAT**: Occasionally found in drift on ocean beaches. **RANGE**: Massachusetts to Texas. **NOTES**: See **Brown-Band Wentletrap** notes.

Krebs' Wentletrap

Krebs' Wentletrap

Epitonium krebsii (Mörch, 1875)

DESCRIPTION: (¾ inch) Aperture subcircular 10 to 12 bladelike costae; 7 to 8 strongly convex whorls. No spiral lines. Spire angle 45 degrees, much broader than in most other wentletraps. **COLOR:** China white, occasionally a trace of brown to pinkish brown on the body whorl. **HABITAT:** In sand from the depth of a few feet to 1,000 feet. **RANGE:** North Carolina to Brazil. Rarely washes ashore. **NOTES:** Rare in North Carolina.

Many-Ribbed Wentletrap

Many-Ribbed Wentletrap

Epitonium multistriatum (Say, 1826)

DESCRIPTION: (½ inch) Small, fragile, high-spired shell with seven or eight whorls. Similar to **Angulate Wentletrap** except smaller and ribs noticeably thinner and closer together. Adult has 16 to 19 ribs on body whorl. Very fine spiral ribbing. Oval aperture with thin lip. **COLOR:** Dull white exterior and interior. **HABITAT:** Occasionally found in drift on ocean beaches. **RANGE:** Massachusetts to Florida and Texas. **NOTES:** See **Brown-Band Wentletrap** notes.

Brown-Band Wentletrap

Brown-Band Wentletrap

Gyroscala rupicola (Kurtz, 1860)

DESCRIPTION: (½ inch) Small shell with a high, sharply pointed spire composed of globose whorls. About 12 to 18 weak ribs on each whorl. Smooth spaces between ribs. Round aperture. Operculum. **COLOR:** Whitish exterior with brown spiral bands. Two brown bands on body whorl. Mahogany operculum. **HABITAT:** Lives in sounds and just offshore. Occasionally washed onto sound and ocean beaches, usually in drift at the tide line. Easily overlooked because of its small size. **RANGE:** Massachusetts to Texas. **NOTES:** Also called a Lined Wentletrap. About 24 species of wentletraps have been recorded in North Carolina waters. A carnivore, it forages in sand for sea anemones and tears tissue with its jaws. It secretes a substance that turns purple and may anesthetize the anemones. Females lays strings of sand-covered egg capsules. Its young are free-swimming. The Precious Wentletrap (up to 2¾ inches long) from the Pacific Ocean is one of the prettiest shells known. **SCIENTIFIC NAME CHANGE:** Previous name: *Epitonium rupicola* (Kurtz, 1860). The species has been reassigned to the genus *Gyroscala.*

....

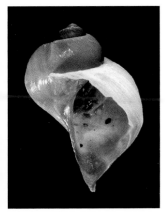

Elongate Janthina

Elongate Janthina

Janthina globosa (Swainson, 1822)

DESCRIPTION: (1 inch) Smooth, fragile shell with about three well-rounded whorls. Large, elliptical aperture. Thin angular lip hangs below whorls. The base of the columella on the inner margin of aperture extends farther downward than in **Janthina**, forming an acutely angular juncture with the outer lip. No umbilicus or operculum. **COLOR:** Top and bottom halves nearly the same shade of violet. Iridescent interior. **HABITAT:** Lives suspended upside down from a raft of bubbles on the ocean surface. Occasionally found on ocean beaches after storms. **RANGE:** Warm Atlantic and Pacific waters; lives in the Gulf Stream. **NOTES:** Also called Globe Violet Snail or Elongate Purple Sea-Snail. See Janthina notes. See plate 16.

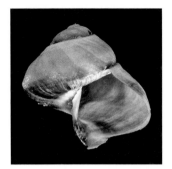

Janthina

....

Janthina

Janthina janthina (Linnaeus, 1758)

DESCRIPTION: (1 inch) Smooth, fragile inflated shell with three or four sloping whorls that are rounded but slightly angular. Large aperture round or elliptical. Thin lip hangs below whorls. The straight columella, or inner margin of aperture, extends downward, forming a rounded intersection with the outer lip. No umbilicus or operculum. COLOR: Top half of shell light purple. Lower half deep purple. Interior not iridescent. HABITAT: Lives suspended upside down from a raft of bubbles on the ocean surface. Sometimes found washed onto beaches after storms. RANGE: Warm Atlantic and Pacific waters. NOTES: Also called a Common Purple Snail or Violet Snail. This carnivore feeds on tiny jellyfish, *Velella* and *Physalia*, and is often found on these creatures. A hermaphrodite; the male stage occurs first. Young males mate with the older individuals that have transformed to females. Young are free-swimming. Adult life is spent in the open ocean, hanging upside down by its foot from a raft of bubbles. It forms the bubbles by trapping air inside mucus with its foot. Its dependence on the currents has resulted in the loss of its ability to move on its own.

Dwarf Wentletrap

....

Dwarf Wentletrap

Opalia pumilio (Mörch, 1875)

DESCRIPTION: (½ inch) Elongate with 10 to 12 whorls, 9 to 15 rounded costae on the body whorl. Outer lip much thickened. Often has former varices on spire. Pitted spiral lines under magnification. COLOR: Nuclear whorls amber. Body whorls grayish white. HABITAT: Just offshore to

depth of 600 feet. Soft substrate. **RANGE:** North
Carolina to Florida and Barbados; also Gulf of
Mexico. **NOTES:** Carnivore. Rarely washes ashore.

....

LITTORINIDAE (PERIWINKLES)

Short, spindle-shaped shell; rounded aperture;
no siphonal canal.

....

Interrupted Periwinkle
Echinolittorina placida (D. Reid, 2009)

Interrupted Periwinkle

DESCRIPTION: (½ inch) Fairly thick and strong with
pear-shaped aperture; 6 to 8 whorls, upper whorls
etched with 10 to 13 fine spiral lines. **COLOR:**
Whitish to bluish-white background with slanting
zigzag stripes of brown or purplish brown, often
with a continuous spiral band of black just above
the suture. Columella brown. **HABITAT:** Upper
intertidal zone in the crevices of rocks, seawalls,
pilings, or other hard surfaces. **RANGE:** Cape
Lookout to both coasts of Florida and the Gulf of
Mexico. **NOTES:** This recently described species
was first reported in the mid-1980s as occurring
sporadically in North Carolina near Fort Fisher
and Wrightsville Beach. Hugh Porter (2008) discovered and reported it (as the Zebra Periwinkle,
Echinolittorina ziczac [Gmelin, 1791]) at several
locations in Carteret County, and it appears to
have become established there. It has expanded
its range from the Gulf of Mexico only within the
past 50 years and was previously considered a
subspecies of the Zebra Periwinkle, which occurs
in Southeastern Florida and the Caribbean.

Marsh Periwinkle

......

Marsh Periwinkle

Littoraria irrorata (Say, 1822)

DESCRIPTION: (1 inch) Small, top-shaped shell. Globe-like body whorl and sharp spire. Spire less than twice the aperture length. Many regular spiral ridges. Round or elliptical aperture. Operculum. **COLOR:** Grayish-cream exterior with reddish streak on inner lip. Spiral cords often with dark, broken bands. Interior not iridescent. **HABITAT:** Lives in brackish marshes and on marsh grass. Frequently found on sound beaches. **RANGE:** New York to Texas. **NOTES:** An herbivore, it scrapes algae from blades of marsh grass with its radula. Females lay floating egg capsules. Young are free-swimming.

NATICIDAE (MOONSNAILS)

Globe-shaped shell; low spire; umbilicus and callus.

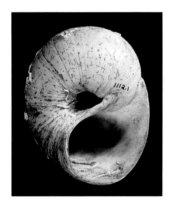

Northern Moonsnail

......

Northern Moonsnail

Euspira heros (Say, 1822)

DESCRIPTION: (4¼ inches) Smooth, globe-shaped shell. Small, deep umbilicus covered only slightly by a button-shaped lobe. Large elliptical aperture. Horny operculum. **COLOR:** Bluish gray with gray umbilicus. Light brown operculum. Yellowish periostracum. **HABITAT:** Occasionally washed onto ocean beaches north of Cape Hatteras. **RANGE:** Canada to Cape Hatteras. **NOTES:** See **Shark Eye** notes. Specimens found on beaches south of Cape Hatteras are probably fossil shells.

Colorful Moonsnail

Colorful Moonsnail
Naticarius canrena (Linnaeus, 1758)

DESCRIPTION: (1¾ inches) Smooth, globe-shaped shell with a small spire. Umbilicus area almost covered by a calcareous pad. Large and elliptical aperture. Calcareous operculum. COLOR: Yellow tan with broad tan or brown spiral bands crossed by narrow dark brown axial zigzags or marks. White umbilicus, calcareous pad, and operculum. Interior not iridescent. HABITAT: Lives offshore. Commonly brought in as bycatch with **Atlantic Calico Scallops**. RANGE: North Carolina to Uruguay. NOTES: Also known as the Colorful Atlantic Natica. See **Shark Eye** notes. SCIENTIFIC NAME CHANGE: Previous name: *Natica canrena* (Linnaeus, 1758). The species has been reassigned to the genus *Naticarius*.

Shark Eye

Shark Eye
Neverita duplicata (Say, 1822)

DESCRIPTION: (3½ inches) Smooth, globe-shaped shell with a small spire. Resembles a shark's eye because line winds around the spire. Umbilicus almost covered by a large, button-like lobe. Large elliptical aperture. Horny operculum. COLOR: Bluish brown or purplish gray with a gray umbilicus, brown callus, and light brown, semitransparent operculum. HABITAT: Lives on mud-sand flats in high-salinity estuaries and offshore. Commonly washed onto sound and ocean beaches. RANGE: Cape Cod, Massachusetts, to Texas. NOTES: Also called an Atlantic Moonsnail. A carnivore, it is a very active predator that burrows rapidly through sand to find prey. It attacks other mollusks, including relatives, by using its radula and acid secretions to drill a beveled hole through the prey's shell. This species leaves wide, flat tracks over sand at low tide. Females lay eggs in "sand collars," which they form out of mucus and sand grains; these can often be found on beaches during the summer. Young are free-swimming.

....

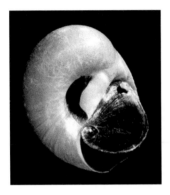

Milk Moonsnail

Milk Moonsnail
Polinices lacteus (Guilding, 1834)

DESCRIPTION: (¾ inch) Solid, ovate, slightly oblong shell with a short spire. Deep, narrow umbilicus partially covered by a button-like callus. Oval aperture with a flattened inner lip. Horny operculum. Thin and smooth periostracum. COLOR: Shiny, milky white exterior. Reddish-brown operculum. Yellowish periostracum. Similar to **White Moonsnail**. HABITAT: Lives in waters just off the southern North Carolina coast. Somewhat commonly found by scuba divers. RANGE: North Carolina to Florida and Brazil. NOTES: See **Shark Eye** notes. This species has a spiral sand collar.

....

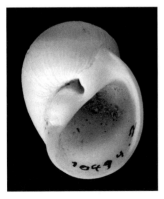

White Moonsnail

White Moonsnail
Polinices uberinus (d'Orbigny, 1842)

DESCRIPTION: (¾ inch) Small, smooth, globe-shaped shell. No spiral cords on whorl. Umbilicus partially covered by a button-shaped lobe. Large elliptical aperture. Horny operculum. COLOR: Glassy white exterior. White callus. Red operculum. HABITAT: Lives offshore. Has been found in **Atlantic Calico Scallop** beds. RANGE: North Carolina to Florida. NOTES: Also called a Dwarf White Moon Shell. See **Shark Eye** notes.

Brown Baby-Ear

Brown Baby-Ear
Sinum maculatum (Say, 1831)

DESCRIPTION: (1¾ inches) Similar to **White Baby-Ear** but not as flat (spire protrudes slightly). Low spiral cords on upper side of whorl. When alive, mantle almost completely surrounds shell. No umbilicus. Large, round aperture. No operculum. COLOR: Light brown streaks on exterior of shell. Mantle spotted with reddish brown. HABITAT: Lives offshore. Was brought in as bycatch with **Atlantic Calico Scallops**. RANGE: North Carolina to Brazil. NOTES: Also called a Maculated Baby-Ear or Spotted Baby-Ear. See **Shark Eye** notes.

White Baby-Ear

White Baby-Ear
Sinum perspectivum (Say, 1831)

DESCRIPTION: (1¾ inches) Flat, smooth, ovate shell. Well named. Low spiral cords on upper side of whorl. When alive, almost completely covered by mantle: resembles a piece of white gristle. No umbilicus. Large, round aperture. No operculum. COLOR: White exterior. Pale brown periostracum. Yellowish-cream mantle. HABITAT: Lives on sand flats in high-salinity estuaries and shallow offshore waters and is commonly washed onto ocean beaches. RANGE: Maryland to Brazil. NOTES: Also called Common Atlantic Baby-Ear. See **Shark Eye** notes.

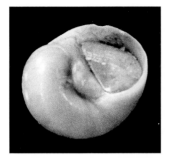

Miniature Moonsnail

....

Miniature Moonsnail

Tectonatica pusilla (Say, 1822)

DESCRIPTION: (¼ inch) Small, stout, oval shell with a short spire. Narrow umbilicus almost covered by a callus. Oval aperture with flattened inner lip. Flattened calcareous operculum. COLOR: Shiny tan exterior. Body whorl with a light brown mid-band of solid or irregular axial markings. HABITAT: Lives just offshore. Occasionally washed onto ocean beaches. RANGE: Maine to Florida and Brazil. NOTES: Frequently found in stomach of the orange-and-blue sea star, *Astropecten articulatus.* See **Shark Eye** notes for feeding habits.

CERITHIOPSIDAE (MINIATURE CERITHS)

Small, elongate, turret shaped; sharply pointed spire; concave base with very short, straight siphonal canal.

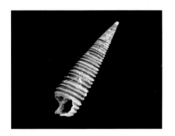

Adam's Miniature Cerith

....

Adam's Miniature Cerith

Seila adamsi (H. C. Lea, 1845)

DESCRIPTION: (⅜ inch) Small, slender shell. Flat whorls, each with three raised spiral threads. About three, smooth, glassy early whorls. Smooth, concave base. Aperture length about one-fifth of total shell length. Short, twisted, open canal. COLOR: Dark brown to orangish brown. HABITAT: Lives offshore to depths of about 100 feet and occasionally on shelly bottoms of high-salinity estuaries such as Bogue Sound and Beaufort Inlet. Commonly washed onto ocean beaches. RANGE: Massachusetts to Florida, Texas, and Brazil. NOTES: Also called a Wood Screw Shell.

EULIMIDAE (EULIMAS)

Small shell with glossy surface; acutely conical with high, pointed spire; small aperture with no siphonal canal.

Conoidal Eulima

Conoidal Eulima

Melanella conoidea (Kurtz and W. Stimpson, 1851)

DESCRIPTION: (¼ inch) Acutely cone-shaped, glossy shell with flat-sided whorls. Angular shoulder and a slightly convex base on body whorl. Finely incised sutures. Elliptical aperture less than one-quarter the total shell length. No umbilicus. COLOR: White to gray, sometimes with some brown. HABITAT: Lives offshore south of Cape Hatteras to depths of about 100 feet. Also lives in high-salinity estuaries such as Back and Bogue Sounds near Beaufort Inlet. Occasionally washed onto ocean beaches and found in drift lines. RANGE: Cape Hatteras to Florida and the Caribbean. NOTES: Also called a Cone-Like Balcis. This species is sometimes hard to pick up because its surface is slick. Parasitic on sea cucumbers, *Holothuria* species. It feeds by sucking blood from the oral or anal end of the host. Often, this species can be found in stomach of the sea star *Astropecten articulatus*.

Cucumber Melanella

Cucumber Melanella

Melanella polita (Linnaeus, 1758)

DESCRIPTION: (½ inch) Similar to **Conoidal Eulima** except the shoulder of the body whorl is rounded instead of angular. **COLOR:** White to gray, sometimes with some brown. **HABITAT:** Same as Conoidal Eulima. **RANGE:** New Jersey to Brazil. **NOTES:** Parasitic on the sea cucumber *Holothuria impatiens*. See Conoidal Eulima notes for feeding technique. **SCIENTIFIC NAME CHANGE:** Porter's original name, *Melanella intermedia* (Cantraine, 1835), is synonymous with *Melanella polita* (Linnaeus, 1758). Having described the shell earlier, Linnaeus's name takes precedence.

Brown-Line Niso

. . . .

Brown-Line Niso

Niso aeglees (K. J. Bush, 1885)

DESCRIPTION: (½ inch) Acutely cone-shaped shell with flat-sided whorls. Angled shoulder of body whorl. Aperture length less than half the total shell length. Broadly ovate aperture. Deep, funnel-like umbilicus. **COLOR:** Shiny, light brown whorls. A narrow dark line on all whorl sutures, the angled shoulder of the body whorl, and the angled shoulder of the umbilicus. May have dark brown axial flammules on whorls. **HABITAT:** Lives offshore south of Cape Hatteras to depths of about 100 feet. Occasionally washed onto ocean beaches. **RANGE:** North Carolina to Texas and Brazil. **NOTES:** Members of this family are parasites, living on echinoderms such as sea stars, sea urchins, sand dollars, and sea cucumbers. The animal has no radula but does have jaws that pierce the echinoderms' skin, allowing the mollusk to extend its mouth into its host. This species is often found in stomach of the sea star *Astropecten articulatus*. See plate 17.

CALYPTRAEIDAE (SLIPPERSNAILS, CUP-AND-SAUCER)

Resembles a boat or slipper, with shelly platform behind the beak within the broad open aperture.

Spiny Slippersnail
Bostrycapulus aculeatus (Gmelin, 1791)

Spiny Slippersnail

DESCRIPTION: (1 inch) Cap-shaped shell with a small shelf or deck underneath. Attaches to rock or shell. North Carolina's only slippersnail with a rough or spiny exterior. **COLOR:** Exterior orange to brown, mottled or rayed with white. Polished, whitish interior mottled or rayed with brown. Whitish shelf or deck. **HABITAT:** Occasionally washed onto ocean beaches south of Cape Hatteras. **RANGE:** North Carolina to Brazil. **NOTES:** Also called a Thorny Slipper Shell. See **Convex Slippersnail** notes. **SCIENTIFIC NAME CHANGE:** Previous name: *Crepidula aculeata* (Gmelin, 1791). The species has been reassigned to the genus *Bostrycapulus*.

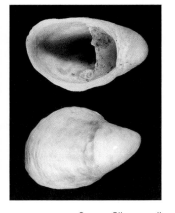

Convex Slippersnail
Crepidula convexa (Say, 1822)

DESCRIPTION: (½ inch) Small, cap-shaped shell with a strong arch and an oval base. A prominent apex curves around like an elf's cap. A shelf or deck underneath is set deep in the shell. Wrinkled exterior. Not found attached to others. **COLOR:** Brownish exterior with specks of reddish brown.

Convex Slippersnail

Reddish-brown interior. **HABITAT:** Lives offshore. Occasionally found on offshore beaches. **RANGE:** Massachusetts to Texas. **NOTES:** This species is a filter feeder. A sequential hermaphrodite, it changes sex during its life cycle, starting out as male and later becoming female. Sex change is influenced by age and by hormones released by the opposite sex. See **Common Atlantic Slippersnail** notes.

Common Atlantic Slippersnail

....

Common Atlantic Slippersnail
Crepidula fornicata (Linnaeus, 1758)

DESCRIPTION: (2½ inches) Slightly arched cap-shaped shell with an oval base. Appearance of a slipper or small boat with a small shelf or deck underneath. Pointed end of the deck not deep in the shell. Smooth or slightly wrinkled exterior. When living, often attached to others. **COLOR:** Buff exterior with small brownish specks. Buff interior sometimes lightly flecked with brown. White shelf. **HABITAT:** Lives offshore. Common on sound and ocean beaches. **RANGE:** Nova Scotia, Canada, to Texas. **NOTES:** Also called a Boat Shell or Quarterdeck. Its shape varies, depending on the shape of the shell to which it attaches. This species is a filter feeder. It may take over oyster beds and smother the mollusks. A sequential hermaphrodite, it often lives in stacks, one on top of another with large females at the bottom and the much smaller males positioned at or near the top. Females produce capsule-like eggs, attach them to a rock, and brood them until they hatch. Veliger larvae are free-swimming.

Spotted Slippersnail

Spotted Slippersnail

Crepidula maculosa (Conrad, 1846)

DESCRIPTION: (1 inch) Similar to the **Common Atlantic Slippersnail** except more heavily spotted. Fairly straight edge on shelf. COLOR: Exterior and interior white to buff with many small, reddish-brown spots. White shelf. HABITAT: Lives offshore near the Gulf Stream on dead penshells. Might be found on ocean beaches. RANGE: North Carolina to Gulf of Mexico. NOTES: See Common Atlantic Slippersnail notes.

Eastern White Slippersnail

Eastern White Slippersnail

Crepidula plana (Say, 1822)

DESCRIPTION: (1½ inches) Cap-shaped flat or concave shell (shape acquired from frequently living inside empty snail shells). Oval to elongate base with a small, convex shelf or deck underneath. Wrinkled exterior with concentric lines. COLOR: White exterior and interior. Glossy interior. HABITAT: Lives in sounds and offshore. Commonly found washed onto sound and ocean beaches. RANGE: Nova Scotia, Canada, to Brazil. NOTES: Also called a Flat Slipper Shell. This species often attaches inside the aperture of dead shells, especially *Busycon* and *Polinices* species (even if a hermit crab is using the dead shell as a home). See also **Common Atlantic Slippersnail** notes.

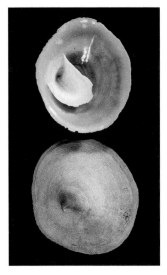

Striate Cup-and-Saucer

Striate Cup-and-Saucer

Crucibulum striatum (Say, 1826)

DESCRIPTION: (1½ inches wide) Cap-shaped shell with round base and a small oval cup on one side of the interior of the shell. Many wavy, radial ridges on exterior. Apex near center and slightly twisted. COLOR: Exterior pinkish gray to yellowish brown. Yellow-brown to orange-brown interior. Shelf or deck white. HABITAT: Lives offshore on hard surfaces, sometimes attached to **Sea Scallops**. Occasionally found on ocean beaches. RANGE: Canada to Brazil. NOTES: Also called a Cup-and-Saucer Limpet. See **Common Atlantic Slippersnail** notes.

CYPRAEIDAE (COWRIES)

Shiny, cylindrical, egg-shaped shell; resembles a lightweight olive shell when immature but transforms at maturity by infolding and thickening the outer lip and lining both inner and outer apertural lips with small, strong, evenly spaced teeth. In life the mantle covers the back of the shell and is retractable into the aperture. Many cultures worldwide used cowries as religious and fertility symbols, and they were a popular form of early money. However, cowries were not readily available in North America, and some Indigenous people here used olive snail shells, whelk shells, and hard clams for currency.

Atlantic Deer Cowrie

Atlantic Deer Cowrie
Macrocypraea cervus (Linnaeus, 1771)

DESCRIPTION: (6 inches) Glossy, smooth, thin, elongate shell with callus covering the spire in the adult. Narrow aperture runs the full length of the shell, with the apertural lips curved and heavily toothed (resembling a mouth with teeth). Large canal-like depression at both ends. No operculum. COLOR: Light to dark brown with many white spots. Color pattern similar to that of a young fawn. Dark brown aperture teeth. HABITAT: Lives offshore on rocks and shipwrecks south of Cape Hatteras. Rarely washed onto ocean beaches. RANGE: Cape Hatteras to Yucatán, Mexico. NOTES: This species feeds at night, but its diet is unknown. Young have brown spiral bands; the spots and aperture teeth appear only when the animals mature. Females lay egg capsules in crevices and protect them with their foot. Young are free-swimming. See plate 18. SCIENTIFIC NAME CHANGE: Previous name: *Cypraea cervus* (Linnaeus, 1771). The species has been reassigned to the genus *Macrocypraea.*

Atlantic Yellow Cowrie

Atlantic Yellow Cowrie
Naria acicularis (Gmelin, 1791)

DESCRIPTION: (¾ inch) Small, glossy, elongate shell with callus over the spire and a narrow aperture the length of the shell. Similar in shape to the **Atlantic Deer Cowrie** but smaller and flatter. Heavily ridged aperture lips (resembling teeth). Large canal-like depression at both ends of aperture. No operculum. COLOR: Yellowish-tan exterior with small yellowish spots. Whitish aperture teeth. HABITAT: Lives offshore in rocky areas or on

wrecks. **RANGE:** Cape Hatteras to Brazil. **NOTES:**
See Atlantic Deer Cowrie notes. **SCIENTIFIC NAME**
CHANGE: Previous name, *Cypraea spurca acicu-*
laris (Gmelin, 1791), is no longer accepted. The
species name *spurca* applies to an East African–
Mediterranean shell only. The subspecies name
acicularis is elevated to valid species status and
reassigned to the genus *Naria.*

....

OVULIDAE (SIMNIAS, CYPHOMAS)

Smooth, glossy, cylindrical shell; resembles a
mouth with smooth lips. Shell growth analogous
to cowries (see family Cypraeidae). Animals live
on whip and fan corals.

....

McGinty's Cyphoma

McGinty's Cyphoma
Cyphoma mcgintyi (Pilsbry, 1939)

DESCRIPTION: (1¼ inches) Smooth, glossy, elongate
shell resembling a pair of lips with no teeth (both
lips of the long, narrow aperture are smooth).
Humped back with one swollen ridge. No spire.
When alive, mantle may completely cover the
shell. No operculum. **COLOR:** Cream shell. Cream
mantle with dark brown spots and occasionally a
pink or lavender tint. When alive, vivid patterns
on shell and mantle. **HABITAT:** Lives south of
Cape Hatteras on sea fans and sea whips in inlets
and offshore. Rarely found on beaches. **RANGE:**
North Carolina to Florida. **NOTES:** Also known
as McGinty's Flamingo Tongue. A carnivore, it
lives and feeds on sea fans and whips. Males are
territorial and defend certain portions of an individual sea fan. Females lay clumps of eggs on the
branches. Young are free-swimming. The more

common Caribbean species *Cyphoma gibbosum* (Linnaeus, 1758) is often used in jewelry.

....

One-Tooth Simnia

Simnialena uniplicata (G. B. Sowerby II, 1849)

DESCRIPTION: (¾ inch) Small, thin, almost cylindrical shell. Smooth, glossy exterior. No spire. Very narrow aperture almost the length of the shell. Open canals at both ends of aperture. Both

One-Tooth Simnia

lips smooth. Several folds on lower part of inner aperture wall. Slightly thickened outer lip. COLOR: Exterior yellow, orange, or occasionally light purple. Network of brown lines on mantle. HABITAT: Lives in inlets and offshore on living sea whips. Rarely found on beaches. RANGE: Virginia to Brazil. NOTES: This species is a carnivore. The shell and mantle color depend on the color of the sea whips it feeds on. Males defend territories on sea whips. Females lay eggs on the branches. Young are free-swimming. See plate 19.

TRIVIIDAE (TRIVIAS)

Small, cylindrical, cowrie-shaped shells; surface resembles corduroy (rows of ridges around shell). Five species in North Carolina; all offshore south of Cape Hatteras and rarely seen on beach.

....

Coffeebean Trivia

Pusula pediculus (Linnaeus, 1758)

DESCRIPTION: (½ inch) Small, globe-shaped shell flattened above, with 16 to 18 cords circling the shell. Small groove down back of the shell.

Coffeebean Trivia

Narrow, toothed aperture extending the length

of the shell. Ornate mantle almost completely covers the shell. **COLOR:** Light brown or pinkish brown with three dark brown patches on the back. **HABITAT:** Lives in deep offshore waters on shipwrecks. Found by scuba divers south of Cape Lookout at 50-foot depths. **RANGE:** Cape Hatteras to Brazil. **NOTES:** It resembles a cowrie shell, but the animal inside is different. A carnivore, it feeds on tunicates. Females deposit egg capsules inside the flesh of tunicates. Young are free-swimming. In Florida, trivias are more common on the beach, and the attractive shell is often used in jewelry. **SCIENTIFIC NAME CHANGE:** Previous name: *Trivia pediculus* (Linnaeus, 1758). The species has been reassigned to the genus *Pusula*.

FICIDAE (FIGSNAILS)

Only one North American species; shell has large body whorl with a crisscross sculptural pattern, surrounding a very flat spire and an elongate aperture that narrows to a long canal.

Atlantic Figsnail
Ficus ficus (Linnaeus, 1758)

DESCRIPTION: (4½ inches) Smooth, pear-shaped shell with almost no spire. Unlike the similar **Pearwhelk**, has many pronounced spiral ridges crossing finer axial riblets and no operculum. Wide aperture on right runs almost the length of the shell and narrows into a long siphonal canal. Spiral ridges or folds inside inner lip. **COLOR:** Cream or pinkish-gray exterior with brown broken spiral stripes. Glossy tan interior. **HABITAT:** Lives offshore. Rarely found on ocean beaches.

Atlantic Figsnail

RANGE: North Carolina to Mexico. NOTES: Also called a Paper Fig Shell. This species is a carnivore. Females lay egg capsules in wide rows. Planktonic veliger larvae. When alive, the mantle almost covers the shell. Do not confuse this shell with the Pearwhelk. SCIENTIFIC NAME CHANGE: Porter's original name, *Ficus communis* (Röding, 1798), is synonymous with *Ficus ficus* (Linnaeus, 1758). Having described the shell earlier, Linnaeus's name takes precedence.

STROMBIDAE (TRUE CONCHS)

Adult shells are thick and heavy with a flared outer lip with a characteristic stromboid notch at the base of the outer lip, near the columella.

Florida Fighting Conch

Florida Fighting Conch
Strombus alatus (Gmelin, 1791)

DESCRIPTION: (4½ inches) Heavy shell with rough exterior surface. Sharply knobbed whorl shoulders. Large aperture with a smooth inner margin. Fold in upper end of aperture running toward interior. Flaring outer lip with a notch (stromboid notch) near the siphonal canal. Sickle-shaped operculum. COLOR: Light to dark brown exterior with shiny, metallic parietal shield that may be dark reddish orange to reddish purple. Similar interior but not metallic. HABITAT: Lives offshore, known at depths up to 120 feet. Occasionally washed onto ocean beaches, particularly Cape Lookout and Shackleford Banks. RANGE: North Carolina to Texas. NOTES: An herbivore, it feeds on red algae. Females lay long, jellylike strings of eggs that release free-swimming veliger larvae.

Occasionally, it is brought up by offshore fishing trawlers. The tasty meat can be eaten as steaks or in chowders and salads. It is closely related to the Queen Conch or Pink Conch (*Aliger gigas* [Linnaeus, 1758]), which is used in conch chowder throughout the Caribbean region. See plate 20.

....

TONNIDAE (TUNS)

Large globose body whorl; lightweight but strong shell covered with spiral ridges; no parietal shield. "Tun" refers to a large cask, or barrel, equal to four hogsheads.

....

Giant Tun

Giant Tun
Tonna galea (Linnaeus, 1758)

DESCRIPTION: (7½ inches) Large, globe-shaped, fragile shell with 19 to 21 broad, flattened, widely spaced spiral ridges. Large aperture surrounds low spire. No operculum on adults. Slightly flared outer lip. Varnish-like periostracum. COLOR: White to brown, sometimes streaked with brown. Tip of spire deep golden brown. HABITAT: Lives offshore. Rarely found on ocean beaches. Occurs on **Atlantic Calico Scallop** beds. RANGE: North Carolina to Argentina. NOTES: A carnivore, it swallows animals whole and secretes acid to digest them. Females lay eggs in wide rows. Young are free-swimming. See plate 21.

BURSIDAE (FROGSNAILS)

Medium-sized short-spired shells, distinctly flattened because the animal produces two stout rows of thickened prior outer lips, or varices, on opposite edges and has a distinctive posterior siphonal canal at the top rear of the aperture and at each varix. Three species in North Carolina, all offshore south of Cape Hatteras and fairly uncommon to rare.

Chestnut Frogsnail

Chestnut Frogsnail
Marsupina bufo (Bruguière, 1792)

DESCRIPTION: (2¼ inches) Shell's shape resembles a small frog. Rough surface with beaded spiral rows. Wide aperture with a deep canal at both ends. Inner lip with spiral ridges running into aperture. Appears flattened because the thick outer lip on right is directly opposite the large thick former varix on left side. Inner and outer lips toothed. Thin operculum. COLOR: Dark brown and tan. HABITAT: Lives offshore. Occasionally found in **Atlantic Calico Scallop** catches. RANGE: Cape Hatteras to Brazil. NOTES: A carnivore, it is thought to anesthetize prey before digesting it. Females lay eggs in clusters on hard surfaces. Free-swimming veliger larvae. SCIENTIFIC NAME CHANGE: Previous name: *Bufonaria bufo* (Bruguière, 1792). The species has been reassigned to the genus *Marsupina*.

CASSIDAE (HELMETS, SCOTCH BONNET)

Large shells with globose body whorl; parietal shield; both aperture lips with teeth; upturned siphonal canal at the end of the columella.

Cameo Helmet

Cameo Helmet

Cassis madagascariensis (Lamarck, 1822)

DESCRIPTION: (10¼ inches) Large helmetlike shell with low spire and a pale parietal shield that is oval to slightly triangular in shape. Body whorl with three or more spiral rows of small-to-medium-sized blunt knobs; largest row has five to nine knobs on the shoulder, with the central knob distinctly larger than the others. Narrow aperture almost length of shell. Teeth on both lips. Small, narrow operculum. COLOR: Body whorl exterior yellowish white with faint tan markings. Large, pale brown or orange parietal shield. White aperture teeth with dark brown between them. Brown interior. HABITAT: Lives offshore, mainly off the Outer Banks near the Gulf Stream. At one time, whole shells were common on Cape Lookout beaches. Now, only occasional pieces are found on ocean beaches south of Cape Hatteras. RANGE: Cape Hatteras to the Caribbean. NOTES: Also called an Emperor Helmet or Queen Helmet. This species is one of the largest helmet shells in the world. A carnivore, it feeds on sea urchins and sand dollars; see **Scotch Bonnet** notes. Free-swimming veliger larvae. See plate 22.

Clench Helmet

Clench Helmet
Cassis madagascariensis spinella (Clench, 1944)

DESCRIPTION: (10½ to 14 inches) Similar to **Cameo Helmet** but usually larger, with about 12 uniformly small knobs on the shoulder of the body whorl; one or two additional spiral rows of smaller knobs are sometimes below shoulder. COLOR: Similar to Cameo Helmet except usually lighter (thinner) shell. HABITAT: Lives offshore on sandy or shelly bottoms to depths of about 120 feet. Frequently brought up by scuba divers and fishing trawlers from **Atlantic Calico Scallop** beds. RANGE: South of Cape Hatteras to Florida. NOTES: Described as a subspecies but now recognized as an ecological form of the Cameo Helmet (*Cassis madagascariensis* [Lamarck, 1822]) found in North Carolina waters. It is one of the largest helmet shells in the world. A carnivore, it feeds on sea urchins and sand dollars; see **Scotch Bonnet** notes. Free-swimming veliger larvae. See plate 23.

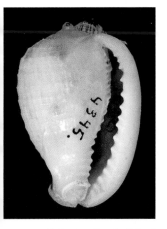

Reticulate Cowrie-Helmet

Reticulate Cowrie-Helmet
Cypraecassis testiculus (Linnaeus, 1758)

DESCRIPTION: (2¾ inches) Inflated, helmetlike shell with a small spire. Narrow aperture almost the length of shell. Axial ribs crossed by spiral grooves, forming a reticulated surface. Smooth parietal shield. Small upper canal and deep, slit-like lower canal on aperture. Inner and outer aperture lips heavily ridged. No operculum in adults. COLOR: Tan-orange exterior with spiral rows of dark brown spots. Orange to white parietal shield and outer lip. Row of dark brown spots also on outer lip. HABITAT: Lives offshore. Rarely washed onto ocean beaches. RANGE: Cape Hatteras to

Brazil. **NOTES:** A carnivore, it feeds on sea urchins and sand dollars; see **Scotch Bonnet** notes.
Females lay eggs in tubelike clumps under stones
and shells. Young are free-swimming. See plate 24.

Scotch Bonnet

....

Scotch Bonnet

Semicassis granulata (Born, 1778)

DESCRIPTION: (3½ inches) Globe-like shell with
short spire and many smooth to occasionally
barred spiral ridges. Light axial cords near shoulder. Occasionally, thickened rib indicates remains
of earlier thick outer lip. Wide aperture with canals at both ends. Thick, toothed outer lip. Inner
lip forms a parietal shield with raised pustules on
lower part. Operculum. **COLOR:** White exterior
with some spiral rows of square, brownish-orange
spots. **HABITAT:** Lives offshore. Shell fragments
common on ocean beaches after storms, but
whole specimens found only occasionally. **RANGE:**
North Carolina to Uruguay. **NOTES:** This species
was declared North Carolina's official seashell by
act of the North Carolina General Assembly in
May 1965 in memory of the state's early Scottish
settlers. North Carolina was the first state to des-
ignate an official seashell. A carnivore, it searches
out and feeds on sea urchins and sand dollars; it
secretes acid to digest them. Females lay eggs in
round "towers" and sit on them. Young hatch as
free-swimming veliger larvae. A closely related
but very rare offshore species, the Coronado
Bonnet (*Echinophoria coronadoi* [Crosse, 1867]),
grows to 3½ inches in length, has several rows of
low knobs near its shoulder, and is a solid brownish tan. See plate 25.

CHARONIIDAE (TRUMPET TRITONS)

Large shell with rounded body whorl and high tapered spire; round to oval aperture with short siphonal canal; outer lip has white teeth in pairs. Only one species in western Atlantic.

Atlantic Trumpet Triton

Charonia variegata (Lamarck, 1816)

DESCRIPTION: (10 inches) Large, graceful, elongate shell with a high spire and wide aperture. Eight or nine whorls on spire. Spire longer than the aperture. Shoulder of the body whorl slightly angular. Small pairs of teeth on outer aperture lip. Ridged inner lip. COLOR: Cream exterior with concentric patterns of brown, purple, or red, suggesting the plumage of a pheasant. Orange interior. On aperture, outer-lip teeth and inner-lip ridges white. HABITAT: Living specimens found by scuba divers off Beaufort Inlet at 60-to-100-foot depths on rocky or shelly substrate near rock outcroppings. RANGE: Cape Hatteras to Florida and Brazil. NOTES: Also called a Trumpet Shell. This species has been known to feed on sea stars and sand dollars. See also **Krebs' Hairy Triton** notes. See plate 26. SCIENTIFIC NAME CHANGE: Previous name, *Charonia tritonis variegata* (Lamarck, 1816), is no longer accepted. *Charonia tritonis* (Linnaeus, 1758) is now recognized as an Indo-Pacific species and *Charonia variegata* as a western Atlantic species. Until recently it was considered a subfamily in family Cymatiidae.

Atlantic Trumpet Triton

CYMATIIDAE (TRITONS)

Five uncommon offshore species of medium-large shells, with large body whorl; ovate to round aperture narrowing to long straight siphonal canal; usually a well-thickened outer lip with apertural teeth and frequently with at least one prominent former varix.

Ringed Triton
Linatella caudata (Gmelin, 1791)

DESCRIPTION: (2¾ inches) Shell with globose body whorl and moderate spire of three to four shouldered whorls. Last whorl slightly shouldered with 18 to 20 strong spiral cords. No axial ribs. Wide near-circular aperture. Smooth inner margin with a slight fold near the lower canal. Outer aperture lip not strongly thickened but slightly flared out. Moderately light, thin shell with thin yellowish periostracum. COLOR: White exterior. Brown periostracum. HABITAT: Lives offshore. RANGE: Virginia to Brazil. NOTES: See Krebs' Hairy Triton notes. SCIENTIFIC NAME CHANGE: Previous name *Cymatium cingulatum* (Lamarck, 1822) is one of several names applied to this shell. *Linatella caudata* (Gmelin, 1791), being the oldest, is therefore the accepted name.

Ringed Triton

Krebs' Hairy Triton
Monoplex krebsii (Mörch, 1877)

DESCRIPTION: (2¾ inches) Shell with a moderately short spire less than twice the aperture length. Whorls of spire joined in a tight coil. Last whorl has six to seven strong spiral cords crossing a regular series of axial ridges. Outer lip of the aperture

Krebs' Hairy Triton

heavily thickened with strong teeth on the outer lip and prominent thickened former varix opposite the aperture. Six to seven strong teeth on outer lip. Two large folds on inner margin and smaller folds running into aperture. Operculum. **COLOR:** White exterior. Light brown periostracum. **HABITAT:** Lives offshore, particularly near **Atlantic Calico Scallop** beds. **RANGE:** North Carolina to the Caribbean. **NOTES:** A carnivore, it anesthetizes its prey with a secretion, then inserts its mouth inside the shell to feed. Females lay small, round egg capsules on hard surfaces. Young are free-swimming. A one-to-two-month swimming stage allows considerable dispersal of the species. Very few tritons have been found in North Carolina waters except during the early 1970s as part of the Atlantic Calico Scallop fishery. See plate 27. **SCIENTIFIC NAME CHANGE:** Previous name, *Cymatium corrugatum krebsii* (Mörch, 1877), is no longer accepted. *Monoplex corrugatus* (Lamarck, 1816) is now recognized as an eastern Atlantic species and *Monoplex krebsii* (Mörch, 1877) as a western Atlantic species.

....

Giant Triton

Monoplex parthenopeus (Salis Marschlins, 1793)

DESCRIPTION: (6 inches) Large shell with rounded body whorl and prominent spiral cords crossing axial ridges. Two strong spiral cords on whorl above the body whorl. Wide oval aperture with a strong inner fold at the upper canal. Spiral ridges on inner lip that run around the columella into the aperture. Thick and knobby outer lip where the spiral cords end. Thick and hairy brown periostracum (as shown). Operculum. **COLOR:** Brownish-yellow exterior with some darker brown

Giant Triton

spiral bands, particularly on the outer lip. Inner margin of aperture orange to reddish brown with white folds. HABITAT: Lives offshore; worn specimens occasionally found on beach. RANGE: North Carolina to Uruguay. NOTES: Also called a Neapolitan Triton. This species is present in Pacific waters as well. See **Krebs' Hairy Triton** notes. It was frequently found in catches of the **Atlantic Calico Scallop** fishery. SCIENTIFIC NAME CHANGE: Previous name: *Cymatium parthenopeum* (Salis Marschlins, 1793). The species has been reassigned to the genus *Monoplex*.

PERSONIDAE (DISTORSIOS)

Two species offshore; round body whorl with large cancellate parietal shield and outer lip surrounding small, distorted and gnarly aperture that narrows to long canal.

Atlantic Distorsio

Atlantic Distorsio
Distorsio clathrata (Lamarck, 1816)

DESCRIPTION: (2¾ inches) Shell somewhat like a triton's but with a distorted appearance and very distinctive aperture. Knobby, checkerboard appearance on surface created by many axial and spiral ribs. Narrow aperture with large canal-like notch on inner lip. Both lips heavily ridged. Large, shiny parietal shield. Hairy periostracum. Small operculum. COLOR: White exterior with some yellow, pink, or brown. Brown satin-like periostracum with some bristles. HABITAT: Lives offshore, south of Cape Hatteras, to 200-foot depths. Rarely washed onto ocean beaches. RANGE: North Carolina to Florida and Brazil. Common bycatch

in the **Atlantic Calico Scallop** fishery. **NOTES:**
Also called a Writhing Shell. See **Krebs' Hairy
Triton** notes. The distorsio's large aperture teeth
and narrow aperture opening give it more pro-
tection from predators than most tritons have.
A similar but even more distorted species, the
McGinty Distorsio (*Distorsio mcgintyi* [W. K.
Emerson and Puffer, 1953]), is occasionally found
farther offshore.

XENOPHORIDAE (CARRIERSNAILS)

One North Carolina species; broadly conical shell;
shape disguised because it is camouflaged by
attachments of shells, rocks, or coral fragments
that the snail cements into its shell during growth;
appears to be a pile of shell debris; aperture
underneath.

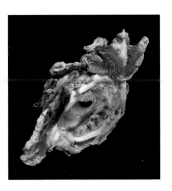

American Carriersnail

American Carriersnail
Xenophora conchyliophora (Born, 1780)

DESCRIPTION: (2¼ inches wide) Top-shaped,
broadly conical shell. Shape rarely seen because
it's covered with attached pieces of shell, stone,
or coral, giving it the appearance of a small pile
of shells or debris. Rounded or elliptical aperture.
COLOR: Yellowish exterior with brown swirls.
Brownish interior. **HABITAT:** Lives offshore. Has
been found in **Atlantic Calico Scallop** beds.
RANGE: North Carolina to Brazil. **NOTES:** Also
called a Common Carrier Shell. This species feeds
on detritus and algae. The family name means
"carrier of strangers." Often called the "original
shell collector." It attaches shells using a special
cement that is sticky underwater. As it grows,

it continues to add shells at its growing edge. Although it is usually assumed that the shell debris is added for camouflage, some investigators think the projections may also help the animal move over the ocean floor.

··

MARGINELLIDAE (MARGINELLAS)

Small, cylindrical shell with narrow aperture extending nearly full length of shell; pear shaped; tiny spire; strong folds on columella; thickened outer lip, frequently with teeth.

·········

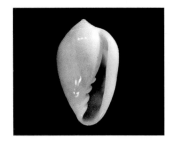

Virginia Marginella

Virginia Marginella
Prunum hartleyanum (Schwengel, 1941)

DESCRIPTION: (½ inch) Tiny, glossy, miniature cowrie-shaped shell with a tiny spire. Narrow aperture almost the length of the shell. Four folds on the columellar portion of the inner lip. Similar to **Seaboard Marginella** except wider and lacks white specks and teeth on the thickened outer lip. No operculum. COLOR: Golden brown exterior, usually with two to three darker spiral bands. White outer lip with two to four brownish spots. Living specimens considerably lighter in color than living specimens of the Seaboard Marginella. HABITAT: Lives near inlets and offshore. RANGE: North Carolina to Florida, offshore in depths up to 120 feet. NOTES: In the previous edition of this book, this species was misidentified as Common Atlantic Marginella (*Prunum apicinum* [Menke, 1828]). A carnivore that can move quickly across the sand. Hatched young crawl away. Hatched young crawl away. Early Native Americans often crafted necklaces from these and similar shells and used them in trading. SCIENTIFIC NAME CHANGE: This species was briefly considered a subspecies of *Prunum virginianum* (Conrad, 1868), which is now recognized as fossil only. The common name Virginia Marginella was previously applied to Conrad's fossil species.

Seaboard Marginella

Seaboard Marginella

Prunum roscidum (Redfield, 1860)

DESCRIPTION: (½ inch) Tiny, glossy shell with a tiny spire and a thickened outer lip in the adult. Very narrow aperture almost the length of shell. Four folds on inner lip. Similar to **Virginia Marginella** but proportionately narrower, with white specks and teeth on the thickened outer aperture lip. No operculum. COLOR: Cream exterior with three brownish spiral bands and a covering of white flecks. Outer lip with four brown spots. HABITAT: Lives near inlets and offshore. Occasionally found on sound and ocean beaches. RANGE: New Jersey to northern Florida. NOTES: Also called a Jersey Marginella. See Virginia Marginella notes. See plate 28. SCIENTIFIC NAME CHANGE: Previous name: *Marginella roscida* (Redfield, 1860). The species has been reassigned to the genus *Prunum*.

VOLUTIDAE (VOLUTES, JUNONIAS)

A large and diverse family, well represented in the Caribbean, with three North Carolina species (two only in very deep water offshore). Elongate cylindrical spotted shell with short spire; narrow aperture extends nearly the full length; strong folds on the columella.

Junonia

. . . .

Junonia

Scaphella junonia (Lamarck, 1804)

DESCRIPTION: (5¼ inches) Spindle-shaped shell with a smooth, shiny surface and spectacular color. Moderate spire. Elongate aperture with short, open lower canal. Four strong folds on columella. Smooth outer lip. No operculum. COLOR: Cream background with large, squarish, reddish-brown to purple spots. HABITAT: Lives offshore in colonies on ocean floor. Rarely washed up after storms on ocean beaches. Sometimes brought in on shrimp boats. RANGE: Cape Hatteras to Texas. NOTES: A carnivore, it feeds on small invertebrates. This species is prized by collectors. It is named for its spots on the shell and mantle, which reminded people in earlier times of the tail of a peacock, the "bird of Juno." See plate 29. SCIENTIFIC NAME CHANGE: Porter attributed the description of Junonia to Shaw, based on information in Tucker Abbott's 1954 edition of *American Seashells.* By the time the second edition was published in 1974, Abbott had revised the attribution to Lamarck, 1804, which is now accepted.

CANCELLARIIDAE (NUTMEGS)

Short, spindle-shaped shell; small aperture; beaded or ribbed; whorls have distinct shoulders; very strong plaits or ridges on the columella. Many members of the family are ectoparasites, feeding on body fluids of other animals.

....

Smith's Nutmeg
Axelella smithii (Dall, 1888)

DESCRIPTION: (½ inch) Small shell with rough surface (axial ribs and spaces between them rough). Seven to nine strong, rounded axial ribs crossed by smaller spiral ridges. Axial ribs generally uniform in size. Oval aperture with open lower canal. Inner lip with spiral ridges running into aperture. Outer lip with cords running into aperture. No operculum. **COLOR:** Brown to brownish red. **HABITAT:** Lives offshore, recorded to about 300-foot depths. Often netted as incidental catch in **Atlantic Calico Scallop** catches. **RANGE:** North Carolina to northern Florida. **NOTES:** See **Common Nutmeg** notes.

Smith's Nutmeg

....

Common Nutmeg
Cancellaria reticulata (Linnaeus, 1767)

DESCRIPTION: (2¼ inches) Rough cancellate surface on shell. Many spiral cords across many axial ribs, resulting in a lattice or beaded pattern. Elongate aperture with short canal. Inner margin with two strong, thin spiral ridges running into aperture (upper ridge stronger than lower ridge). No operculum. **COLOR:** Banded or splotched with cream and orange or brown. **HABITAT:** Lives offshore. Occasionally washed onto ocean beaches. **RANGE:** North Carolina to Brazil. **NOTES:** This species is probably carnivorous because its long proboscis and radula are ideal for feeding on soft-bodied animals.

Common Nutmeg

BUSYCONIDAE (WHELKS)

Large carnivorous gastropods with low spire, large body whorl, and elongate aperture that narrows to a long canal; most with shouldered whorls. This family is restricted to the western Atlantic from Massachusetts to the Yucatán in Mexico, with a strong fossil record and with several species exhibiting considerable variability in shell form and color. The family recently underwent taxonomic revision (Petuch et al., 2015). Harvested commercially, local (Carteret County) fishermen refer to the larger whelk species collectively as "conchs" and make a delicious conch chowder not unlike that made from Queen Conch, a true conch, in the Caribbean region. See notes for Florida Fighting Conch.

Knobbed Whelk

Knobbed Whelk
Busycon carica (Gmelin, 1791)

DESCRIPTION: (11¼ inches) Large, pear-shaped shell. Very similar to the **Lightning Whelk** except for more prominent knobs on the whorl shoulders and aperture on the right (left-handed specimens reported very rarely). Smooth exterior. Wide aperture ends in a long canal. Smooth inner lip. Horny operculum. COLOR: Grayish exterior. Young specimens streaked with purple. Interior solid or blotched with yellow, orange, red, or brown. HABITAT: Lives in sounds, inlets, and shallow offshore waters. Frequently found on sound and ocean beaches. RANGE: Massachusetts to Florida. NOTES: This animal is a carnivore (a major clam predator) and scavenger. It uses its strong foot and aperture lip to force apart bivalves or to chip away the shell until it can insert its mouth and feed on the mollusk inside. Females lay long strings of disk-shaped egg capsules, which are often found washed onto beaches and mistaken for seaweed. Juveniles crawl out of capsules. Note egg capsules in the photo. See plate 30.

....

Kiener's Whelk

Kiener's Whelk

Busycon carica eliceans (Montfort, 1810)

DESCRIPTION: (8 inches) Heavy, rough-looking shell very similar to the **Knobbed Whelk**. Distinguished by a noticeable swelling near the lower part of the body whorl, more outwardly reflected apertural lip, and heavy, recurved spines on the shoulder. COLOR: Gray with brownish-purple axial streaks. Inside aperture lip sometimes glazed orange. HABITAT: Lives on sandy bottoms of sounds, inlets, and shallow offshore waters. Occasionally washed onto ocean beaches south of Cape Fear; found offshore by scuba divers. RANGE: Cape Lookout to Florida. NOTES: Now accepted as a subspecies of *Busycon carica*. See Knobbed Whelk notes for feeding technique and egg capsules.

....

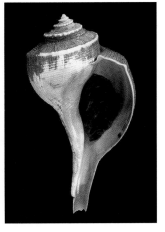

Channeled Whelk

Channeled Whelk

Busycotypus canaliculatus (Linnaeus, 1758)

DESCRIPTION: (8½ inches) Large, pear-shaped shell with aperture on the right. ("Left-handed" specimens, though rare, occur more frequently than in other whelk species.) Fine spiral ridges. Whorl shoulders lack large knobs (shoulders of the earliest whorls beaded). Named for squarish channel at the juncture of each previous whorl. Spire higher than that of the **Pearwhelk**. Wide aperture ends in a long siphonal canal. Smooth inner lip. Horny operculum. COLOR: Yellowish-white to grayish exterior. Interior shades of yellow, orange, or violet. HABITAT: Lives in shallow off-shore waters and the deeper areas of sounds and inlets. Occasionally found on sound and ocean beaches. RANGE: Massachusetts to Florida. NOTES: This species is a carnivore and scavenger. See **Knobbed Whelk** notes for feeding technique and egg capsules. See plate 31.

....

Pearwhelk

Pearwhelk

Fulguropsis pyruloides rachelcarsonae (Petuch, Myers, and Berschauer, 2016)

DESCRIPTION: (5¼ inches) Large, pear-shaped shell with aperture on right. Very similar to the **Atlantic Figsnail**, but with no crisscross sculpture and slightly higher spire. Exterior covered with fine spiral lines, growing stronger toward the tip of the siphonal canal. No knobs on early whorl shoulders, which are more sloping than those of the **Knobbed Whelk**. Each succeeding whorl joins previous whorl just beneath the shoulder; on the **Channeled Whelk**, each whorl forms a sunken channel before attaching to the preceding whorl. Inner aperture lip smooth. Horny operculum. COLOR: Cream with broad, brown, spiral bands crossed by thin brown axial streaks. HABITAT: Lives offshore. RANGE: Cape Hatteras to Florida. NOTES: Also known as the Fig Whelk, but this species should not be confused with the Atlantic Figsnail. It is a carnivore and probably a scavenger. See Knobbed Whelk notes for feeding technique and egg capsules. SCIENTIFIC NAME CHANGE: Previous name: *Busycotypus spiratus* (Lamarck, 1816). The species has been reassigned to the genus *Fulguropsis*, and its previous subspecies (*pyruloides*) has been elevated to full species status and then split into two subspecies: *pyruloides* (Say, 1822) in the Gulf of Mexico and *rachelcarsonae* on the East Coast. This subspecies is named for famed conservationist author Rachel Carson, who often visited and wrote about the coastal ecology of North Carolina.

....

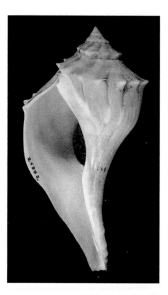

Lightning Whelk

Lightning Whelk

Sinistrofulgur sinistrum (Hollister, 1958)

DESCRIPTION: (12½ inches) Large, pear-shaped shell. Almost a mirror image of the **Knobbed Whelk** (sinistral: coiled counterclockwise when viewed from the top, making them left-handed; whereas a shell that is dextral is coiled clockwise when viewed from the top, making it right-handed); whorl knobs smaller and aperture on the left (remember: lightning = left; right-handed specimens very rare.) Smooth exterior. Wide aperture ends in a long, straight canal. Smooth inner lip. Horny operculum. COLOR: Large specimens (more than 8 to 9 inches) usually dull white on the exterior. Smaller specimens light brown and vertically streaked with darker violet brown. Yellow to violet tints sometimes in interior (Knobbed Whelks usually more orange). HABITAT: Lives on the sandy bottoms of high-salinity sounds and inlets and just offshore. Frequently found on sound and ocean beaches. RANGE: Cape Hatteras to Florida and northeastern Gulf of Mexico. NOTES: See Knobbed Whelk notes for feeding technique and egg capsules. Recent taxonomic studies have shown that a very similar species, *Sinistrofulgur laeostoma* (Kent, 1982), is also resident on the East Coast, ranging from New Jersey to North Florida, and equally or more likely to be encountered in North Carolina than *Sinistrofulgur sinistrum*. Also sinistral, this shell is slightly more robust than *Sinistrofulgur sinistrum*, with a relatively shorter columella and siphonal canal. Specimens of *Sinistrofulgur laeostoma* from the northern part of their range are all white and known as Snow Whelks. The name Lightning Whelk, however, has been in general usage for both of these very similar species throughout North Carolina and in the southern part of their range. **SCIENTIFIC NAME CHANGE:** Previous name: *Busycon sinistrum* (Hollister, 1958). All the sinistral whelk species have been reassigned to the genus *Sinistrofulgur*.

....

COLIDAE (COLUS)

An Arctic group of short, spindle-shaped whelk-like mollusks occurring in cold deeper waters mainly north of Cape Hatteras and/or well off the shelf edge. Shell generally white with small oval aperture; well-developed spire; smooth inner aperture lip.

....

Stimpson's Colus
Colus stimpsoni (Mörch, 1868)

DESCRIPTION: (4½ inches) Spindle-shaped shell resembles an all-white tulip shell. Fragile shell with a rough exterior sculptured by fine spiral lines. Whorls not shouldered. Open upper canal on oval aperture. Tough periostracum. **COLOR:** Chalky white exterior. White interior. Dark brown periostracum. **HABITAT:** Lives offshore, north of Cape Hatteras. Generally found only by deep-water trawlers, particularly those fishing for lobster and

Stimpson's Colus

Sea Scallops. **RANGE:** Labrador, Canada, to North Carolina. **NOTES:** A carnivore and scavenger, it has radulae that efficiently tear dead animal flesh.

....

COLUMBELLIDAE (DOVESNAILS)

Small, spindle-shaped shell with pointed spires longer than aperture; very short, straight siphonal canal; eggs hatch into free-swimming veliger larvae.

....

Lunar Dovesnail

Lunar Dovesnail
Astyris lunata (Say, 1826)

DESCRIPTION: (⅛ inch) Very small, oval shell (elongate yet plump) with a sharp spire. Flat-sided spire about as long as the aperture. Smooth whorls except for spiral lines on the body whorl base. Small, pointed, and translucent early whorls. Elliptical aperture with a short canal at one end. Four small ridges on outer lip. **COLOR:** Shiny cream to gray with many brown or reddish-brown zigzag axial stripes on each whorl. **HABITAT:** Lives in the intertidal zone, just offshore and in eelgrass in high-salinity estuaries. Often found crawling over seaweed, shell, and sand. Commonly found on sound and ocean beaches. Abundant in eelgrass and widgeon-grass beds (*Zostera* and *Ruppia*). **RANGE:** Massachusetts to Florida, Texas, and Brazil. **NOTES:** A carnivore, it preys on small invertebrates attached to the bottom. **SCIENTIFIC NAME CHANGE:** Previous name: *Mitrella lunata* (Say, 1826). The species has been reassigned to the genus *Astyris*.

Greedy Dovesnail

Greedy Dovesnail
Costoanachis avara (Say, 1822)

DESCRIPTION: (½ inch) Small, spindle-shaped shell with rough surface. Convex whorls. About 12 smoothly rounded axial ribs on upper body whorl, becoming less noticeable on earlier whorls. Spire only slightly longer than aperture. Elongate aperture with open lower canal. Outer lip weakly toothed. Small operculum. COLOR: Gray to brownish yellow with whitish dots. HABITAT: Common on shallow-water sand flats and shell-hash bottoms in high-salinity sounds, inlets, and just offshore. Occasionally found on sound and ocean beaches. RANGE: New Jersey to Brazil. NOTES: This species is probably a carnivore or scavenger. Females lay pyramid-shaped eggs on seaweed. Young are free-swimming. SCIENTIFIC NAME CHANGE: Previous name: *Anachis avara* (Say, 1822). The species has been reassigned to the genus *Costoanachis*.

Florida Dovesnail

Florida Dovesnail
Costoanachis floridana (Rehder, 1939)

DESCRIPTION: (½ inch) Almost identical to the **Greedy Dovesnail**, it differs primarily by having finer axial ribbing restricted to the body whorl (no axial ribbing on the early whorls) and the apertural length markedly shorter than the spire height. COLOR: Similar to Greedy Dovesnail. HABITAT: Known in Beaufort Inlet and nearby at 5-to-6-foot depths in the mouth of the Newport River. RANGE: North Carolina to Florida and Texas. NOTES: Also called a Florida Dove Shell. SCIENTIFIC NAME CHANGE: Previous name: *Anachis floridana* (Rehder, 1939). The species has been reassigned to the genus *Costoanachis*.

Well-Ribbed Dovesnail

....

Well-Ribbed Dovesnail

Cotonopsis lafresnayi (P. Fischer and Bernardi, 1857)

DESCRIPTION: (½ inch) Similar to the **Greedy Dovesnail** except straight-sided instead of convex whorls; taller spire; and stronger, straighter, and more numerous (15 to 20) axial ribs that are noticeably crossed by spiral cords. Aperture less than half the total shell length. **COLOR:** Gray to brownish yellow. **HABITAT:** Lives in near-offshore waters. Found washed onto sound and ocean beaches. **RANGE:** Maine to Texas and Yucatán, Mexico. **NOTES:** This species is a carnivore. Female lays volcano-shaped egg capsules on hard surfaces. Young are free-swimming. **SCIENTIFIC NAME CHANGE:** Previous name: *Anachis lafresnayi* (P. Fischer and Bernardi, 1857). The species has been reassigned to the genus *Cotonopsis*.

Fat Dovesnail

....

Fat Dovesnail

Parvanachis obesa (C. B. Adams, 1845)

DESCRIPTION: (¼ inch) Small, robust, spindle-shaped shell with numerous sharp axial ribs. Aperture length about equal to spire height. Slightly thickened outer lip. **COLOR:** Grayish tan. **HABITAT:** Common in sandy, shelly bottoms in high-salinity sounds and near inlets to offshore. **RANGE:** Virginia to Brazil. **NOTES:** Commonly found in beach drift.

FASCIOLARIIDAE (TULIPS, HORSE CONCH)

Large, graceful, spindle-shaped shell, elongate spire; large body whorl; aperture narrows to a long canal. Clusters of fan-shaped egg cases protect young through larval stages; hatchlings crawl away.

Banded Tulip

Banded Tulip
Cinctura hunteria (G. Perry, 1811)

DESCRIPTION: (4½ inches) Medium large spindle-shaped shell resembling the **True Tulip** except smaller. Smooth and shiny exterior. Smooth sutures between whorls. High spire. Teardrop-shaped aperture with fold at the upper canal and one or two folds on the lower inner portion. Horny operculum. COLOR: Cream background mottled with brown (or sometimes with gray or blue green). Thin, dark brown lines spiraling around shell do not run into aperture. HABITAT: Lives in sounds and offshore, frequently on pilings or shelly substrate and oyster beds. Occasionally found on sound and ocean beaches. Dead shells often found occupied by hermit crabs. RANGE: North Carolina to Texas. NOTES: Much more common in North Carolina than the True Tulip. A carnivore, it actively searches for other mollusks. It prefers gastropods, such as the **Atlantic Oyster Drill**, but it will eat bivalves. It uses its foot to pry open bivalves, then wedges its aperture lip inside to feed on the animal's soft parts. Females lay eggs in funnel-shaped capsules attached to rocks or shells. Hatched young crawl away. Offshore, associated with the **Atlantic Calico Scallop** beds, a closely related species, *Cinctura keatonorum*

(Petuch, 2013), thrives. This species, long considered by collectors to be an offshore variant of the Banded Tulip, is distinguished most easily by its color: pale salmon orange, with deeper red-orange flammule-shaped blotches irregularly over the surface. But it is slightly more slender and further distinguished by differences in the fine sculptural detail of the postnuclear whorls and the siphonal canal. See plate 32. **SCIENTIFIC NAME CHANGE**: Previous name, *Fasciolaria lilium hunteria* (G. Perry, 1811), is no longer accepted. The subspecies *hunteria* has been given full species status and reassigned to the genus *Cinctura*.

....

True Tulip

True Tulip

Fasciolaria tulipa (Linnaeus, 1758)

DESCRIPTION: (9½ inches) Large, spindle-shaped shell resembling the **Banded Tulip** but larger, with rough sutures between whorls. Rough spiral cords just below sutures. Smooth and shiny exterior. High spire. Teardrop-shaped aperture with a fold at the upper canal and one or two folds on the lower columella. Horny operculum. **COLOR**: Cream to pink to reddish background with brown spiral bands and many darker and broken spiral lines running into aperture. **HABITAT**: Lives offshore. Live specimens found in Cape Lookout Bight. **RANGE**: North Carolina to Brazil. **NOTES**: A carnivore, it actively searches for mollusks, especially large gastropods. Females lay eggs in funnel-shaped capsules attached to rocks or shells. Hatched young crawl away. See plate 33.

Horse Conch

Horse Conch

Triplofusus giganteus (Kiener, 1840)

DESCRIPTION: (16¼ inches) Large, spindle-shaped shell resembling a tulip shell. Rough exterior surface with low spiral ridges and low axial ribs, covered by a flaky periostracum. Large aperture with a long lower canal. Twisted spiral ridges on columella run into the interior. Large, horny operculum. COLOR: Cream or orange exterior and interior. Exterior covered with a dark brown periostracum (dark orange, red, or brown on small specimens). HABITAT: Lives offshore and on jetties in high-salinity estuaries. Rarely washed onto ocean beaches. RANGE: North Carolina to Mexico. NOTES: One of the largest living gastropods, this species is known to reach more than 19 inches in length. The meat is orange and peppery tasting. A carnivore, it feeds on large gastropods (its favorite prey) while holding the victim's operculum to prevent it from closing. Females lay groups of funnel-shaped, ridged egg capsules, each about 1 inch long. Hatched young crawl away. This species is closely related to tulip shells. It was named Florida's state shell in 1969. SCIENTIFIC NAME CHANGE: Previous name: *Pleuroploca gigantea* (Kiener, 1840). The species has been reassigned to the genus *Triplofusus*.

NASSARIIDAE (MUDSNAILS, NASSAS, DOG WHELKS, BASKET SHELLS)

Small, spindle-shaped shell; small aperture usually less than half total shell length; finely to coarsely beaded surface. Predators and scavengers; eggs hatch directly into veliger larvae.

Eastern Mudsnail

Eastern Mudsnail
Ilyanassa obsoleta (Say, 1822)

DESCRIPTION: (½ inch) Small shell with a slightly rough surface. Weak spiral and axial ribs producing a finely beaded appearance. Lower canal on oval aperture. Smooth inner lip with a parietal shield. Outer lip thin and smooth. COLOR: Chalky white exterior, nearly always covered by a dark brown periostracum. Solid blackish-brown parietal shield. HABITAT: Lives in muddy intertidal zones of sounds and estuaries of moderate salinity. Common on sound and ocean beaches. RANGE: Canada to Florida. NOTES: Also known by a number of common names. Often occurs in very large numbers and helps keep mud flats clean by consuming decaying flesh. An omnivore, it is commonly considered a scavenger because it is quickly attracted to the odor of dead animals, but this species also eats microscopic plants and sometimes live animals. It has a specialized rod to aid in digestion. Females lay rows of funnel-shaped egg capsules with zigzag ridges on seaweed, shells, or rocks. Young hatch as free-swimming veligers.

Threeline Mudsnail

Threeline Mudsnail
Ilyanassa trivittata (Say, 1822)

DESCRIPTION: (¾ inch) Small shell with rough surface. Spiral lines equally strong as axial ribbing, resulting in delicately beaded whorls. Shouldered whorls. Oval-shaped aperture with a canal at both ends. Smooth inner lip and scalloped outer lip. Small parietal shield. Thinner shell with higher spire than in other nassas; aperture much less than half shell length. COLOR: Exterior whitish to yellowish gray, sometimes with brownish bands.

HABITAT: Occasionally washed onto ocean beaches or netted as incidental catch by offshore fishing boats. RANGE: Nova Scotia, Canada, to northern Florida. NOTES: Also called a number of common names. A scavenger, it may also feed on moonsnail eggs. Young are free-swimming.

....

Sharp Nassa

Sharp Nassa

Nassarius acutus (Say, 1822)

DESCRIPTION: (½ inch) Small conical shell, more slender than in other nassas, with a moderately high spire (nearly two-thirds the total shell length). Many axial ribs crossed by two spiral cords on whorls producing a coarsely knobby surface on the spire. Inner aperture lip usually thick and crenulated. Short, open siphonal canal and sometimes a small back canal at top of aperture. Lacks the enameled parietal shield on most nassas. COLOR: Exterior white to creamish. On fresh specimens, a brown spiral thread may connect the knobs. HABITAT: Known living in intertidal areas of the Cape Fear area. Common on shell-hash bottoms in shallow sound waters near inlets. Occasionally found on ocean beaches. RANGE: North Carolina to Florida and Texas. NOTES: Also called a Sharp-Knobbed Nassa, Sharp-Knobbed Dog Whelk, or Narrow Basket Shell. A scavenger, it is reported to feed on mollusk egg capsules.

....

White Nassa
Phrontis alba (Say, 1826)

White Nassa

DESCRIPTION: (½ inch) Small robust shell with rough surface. Strong, rounded axial ribs crossed by many weaker spiral lines. Round aperture with a canal at both ends. Thick outer lip. Parietal shield not well developed. COLOR: White to yellowish exterior, sometimes with light brown spiral lines. White parietal shield. HABITAT: Lives offshore. Was brought in with catches of **Atlantic Calico Scallops**. RANGE: North Carolina to Brazil. NOTES: Also called a Variable Nassa, Variable Dog Whelk, or White Basket Shell. This species is a scavenger. Young are free-swimming. SCIENTIFIC NAME CHANGE: Previous name: *Nassarius albus* (Say, 1826). The species has been reassigned to the genus *Phrontis*.

....

Bruised Nassa
Phrontis vibex (Say, 1822)

Bruised Nassa

DESCRIPTION: (½ inch) Small robust shell with rough surface. Equal spiral and axial ribs, resulting in about 12 ridges and a coarsely beaded surface. Flattened whorls. Elongate aperture with canal at both ends. Aperture nearly half the shell length. Smooth inner lip with prominent parietal shield and thick and toothed outer lip in adults. Juveniles have thin lips and lack the shield. COLOR: Grayish-brown exterior, sometimes with brown bands or mottling. Prominent cream parietal shield. HABITAT: Very common on shallow-water mud-sand flats, on oyster beds, in sounds and inlets, and just offshore. Frequently found on sound and ocean beaches. RANGE: Massachusetts to Brazil. NOTES: Also called a Common Eastern

Nassa, Mottled Dog Whelk, or Bruised Basket Shell. A scavenger, it also has been observed feeding on eggs of marine worms. Females lay thin, oval egg capsules on seaweed, shells, and rocks. Young hatch into free-swimming veliger larvae. SCIENTIFIC NAME CHANGE: Previous name: *Nassarius vibex* (Say, 1822). The species has been reassigned to the genus *Phrontis*.

PISANIIDAE (CANTHARUS)

Until recently a subfamily in the family Buccinidae (whelks), now sometimes called false tritons or false drills. Medium-sized, generally short, spindle-shaped shell; well-developed spire; small ovate aperture; smooth inner aperture lip; short siphonal canal. Larval development and metamorphosis occurs within encapsulated eggs, and the hatched young crawl away.

Tinted Cantharus

Tinted Cantharus
Gemophos tinctus (Conrad, 1846)

DESCRIPTION: (1¼ inches) Spindle-shaped shell with rough surface. Surface sculpture of broad axial ribs crossed by strong spiral ridges. Round aperture with a short canal at both ends. Smooth inner lip. Thick outer lip with many teeth. COLOR: Exterior mottled brown, gray, and cream. Interior white but occasionally with some brown blotches. HABITAT: Lives offshore and on rock jetties and pilings in high-salinity estuaries near inlets. Occasionally found on ocean beaches. RANGE: North Carolina to Brazil. NOTES: Also called a Gaudy Lesser Whelk. A carnivore, it feeds on small mollusks, worms, and barnacles. See also **Florida Rocksnail** notes. SCIENTIFIC NAME CHANGE: Previous name: *Pisania tinctus* (Conrad, 1846). The species has been reassigned to the genus *Gemophos*.

....

Ribbed Cantharus

Hesperisternia multangulus (Philippi, 1848)

DESCRIPTION: (1½ inches) Rough exterior. Axial ribs large and equal in size but squarer than those on the **Caribbean Coralsnail**. Spiral cords on ribs. Angular whorl shoulders. Wide aperture, about half the total length of the shell, ends in a short siphonal canal. Smooth inner margin with a spiral rib near the base. Horny operculum. COLOR: Cream-orange exterior, usually with some brownish specks. HABITAT: Lives offshore. Associated with **Atlantic Calico Scallops**. RANGE: North Carolina to the Caribbean. NOTES: Also called a False Drill. A carnivore, it probably feeds on small mollusks and barnacles below the low-tide line. Females lay funnel-shaped egg capsules with spiny ridges around the top. Hatched young crawl away. See plate 34. SCIENTIFIC NAME CHANGE: Previous name: *Cantharus multangulus* (R. A. Philippi, 1848). The species has been reassigned to the genus *Hesperisternia*.

Ribbed Cantharus

....

MURICIDAE (MUREXES, DRILLS, ROCKSNAILS, CORALSNAILS)

Large body whorl; thick shell; outer lip and previous varices often thickened and bearing prominent spines; inner aperture wall smooth; siphonal canal narrow and sometimes covered with a thin flange extending from the columella. Larval development and metamorphosis occur within encapsulated eggs and the young crawl away.

....

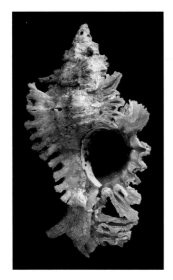

Lace Murex

Lace Murex

Chicoreus florifer (Reeve, 1846)

DESCRIPTION: (2¾ inches) Rough exterior. Three equally spaced axial ribs with long, lacelike spines stronger than intervening ribs. Spiral cords. Wide aperture with a long, slit-like lower canal. Smooth inner lip. Horny operculum. COLOR: Cream or light brown exterior, sometimes with fine darker brown spiral lines. Pinkish apex. HABITAT: Lives offshore. Has been found associated with **Atlantic Calico Scallop** beds. RANGE: North Carolina to the Caribbean. NOTES: A carnivore, it bores holes into bivalve shells and feeds on the soft parts. Females lay egg capsules under rocks and on shells in early summer. Hatched young crawl away. SCIENTIFIC NAME CHANGE: Previous name, *Chicoreus florifer dilectus* (A. Adams, 1855), is no longer accepted. It is synonymous with and replaced by the name *Chicoreus florifer* (Reeve, 1846).

Caribbean Coralsnail

Caribbean Coralsnail
Coralliophila caribaea (Abbott, 1958)

DESCRIPTION: (1 inch) Rough exterior. Large axial ribs equal in size crossed by low coarse spiral ridges. Whorls with sloping angular shoulders. Wide aperture, more than half the total length of shell, ends in a short, slit-like lower canal. Smooth inner margin. Pointed apex. COLOR: Frosty or chalky white exterior. Interior sometimes violet. Reddish operculum. HABITAT: Lives offshore on corals. Has been found associated with **Atlantic Calico Scallop** beds. RANGE: North Carolina to Brazil. NOTES: Also called a Caribbean Coral Shell. This species may resemble a **Ribbed Cantharus**. It is probably a carnivore. Members of this family have no radula. They feed on the coral and sea fans that they live among. Females brood their egg capsules within their mantle cavities until well-developed veligers emerge for a brief planktonic phase prior to final metamorphosis.

Staircase Coralsnail

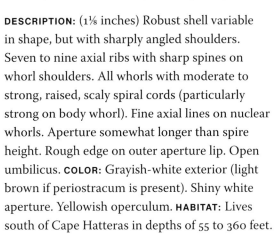

Staircase Coralsnail
Coralliophila scalariformis (Lamarck, 1822)

DESCRIPTION: (1⅛ inches) Robust shell variable in shape, but with sharply angled shoulders. Seven to nine axial ribs with sharp spines on whorl shoulders. All whorls with moderate to strong, raised, scaly spiral cords (particularly strong on body whorl). Fine axial lines on nuclear whorls. Aperture somewhat longer than spire height. Rough edge on outer aperture lip. Open umbilicus. COLOR: Grayish-white exterior (light brown if periostracum is present). Shiny white aperture. Yellowish operculum. HABITAT: Lives south of Cape Hatteras in depths of 55 to 360 feet.

Associated with coral formations. Collected by scuba divers near the shipwreck of *John D. Gill* and on other wrecks near Cape Hatteras. **RANGE:** North Carolina to Florida and the Caribbean. **NOTES:** Also called a Pagoda Coral Shell. This species may be confused with the **Ribbed Cantharus**. See **Caribbean Coralsnail** notes for feeding and reproductive strategies.

. . . .

Thick-Lip Drill

Thick-Lip Drill

Eupleura caudata (Say, 1822)

DESCRIPTION: (1½ inches) Rough exterior with strong spiral lines and large axial ribs. The outer lip and the previous varix are much thicker and stronger than the other axial ribs, giving the shell a somewhat flattened appearance. Sharply angled shoulders on whorl. Wide aperture with a long lower canal. Smooth inner lip. Outer lip thick and toothed. Operculum. **COLOR:** White exterior. Occasionally whorls have several purple spiral bands. **HABITAT:** Lives in sounds and inlets and just offshore, usually near oyster beds, on shelly substrate. Frequently found on sound and ocean beaches. **RANGE:** Massachusetts to Florida. **NOTES:** Also called a Thick-Lipped Oyster Drill. A carnivore, it feeds on oysters and other mollusks. This species is a major oyster predator farther north. In late winter and spring, females lay eggs in slender funnel-shaped capsules that have a slender stalk. Hatched young crawl away.

Pitted Murex

....

Pitted Murex

Favartia cellulosa (Conrad, 1846)

DESCRIPTION: (¾ inch) Similar to **Lightweight Murex** except shoulders of the large axial ribs lack spines, and spaces between the large, rounded ribs are not smooth but crossed by about five scaly cords, giving the surface a pitted appearance. COLOR: Light grayish-pink to light brown exterior. HABITAT: Lives offshore near **Atlantic Calico Scallop** beds. Found by scuba divers. RANGE: North Carolina to Gulf of Mexico and Brazil. NOTES: A carnivore, it is thought to feed on small, thin-shelled bivalves. It probably has crawl-away young.

....

Lightweight Murex

Favartia levicula (Dall, 1889)

DESCRIPTION: (¾ inch) Small shell. Five or more large axial ribs with erect frond-like spines. Shoulder spines curved upward like a hook. Smooth spaces between ribs. Wide aperture with lower canal that is a long slit. Smooth inner lip. Operculum. COLOR: Light brown exterior. HABITAT: Known living offshore in **Atlantic Calico Scallop** beds. RANGE: North Carolina to Florida. NOTES: This species may be easily overlooked because of its small size. It probably has crawl-away young. SCIENTIFIC NAME CHANGE: Previous name: *Murexiella levicula* (Dall, 1889). The species has been reassigned to the genus *Favartia*.

Lightweight Murex

Giant Eastern Murex

Giant Eastern Murex
Hexaplex fulvescens (G. B. Sowerby II, 1834)

DESCRIPTION: (7 inches) Very large, heavy shell with rough surface. Six to 10 axial ribs on each whorl bearing prominent, erect spines. Raised spiral ridges between axial ribs. Long lower canal on aperture nearly closed by smooth flat extension from columella. Smooth inner lip. Heavy operculum. COLOR: Exterior white, yellow brown, or gray with fine purple spiral lines. Interior white and porcelaneous. Dark operculum. HABITAT: Lives offshore, particularly near **Atlantic Calico Scallop** beds. Very rarely washes ashore. RANGE: Cape Hatteras to Texas. NOTES: Also called a Tawny Murex. A carnivore, it feeds on bivalves. Females lay large numbers of egg capsules in single-layer mats on hard surfaces (frequently on other Giant Eastern Murex shells). Has crawl-away young. See plate 35. SCIENTIFIC NAME CHANGE: Previous name: *Muricanthus fulvescens* (G. B. Sowerby II, 1834). The species has been reassigned to the genus *Hexaplex*.

Apple Murex

Apple Murex
Phyllonotus pomum (Gmelin, 1791)

DESCRIPTION: (3½ inches) Medium-large, very robust shell with beaded spiral cords making rough surface. Three axial ribs (varices) are stronger than other ribs and have short spines. Rough spiral cords. Wide, circular aperture with long, slit-like canal that is nearly closed. Smooth inner lip. Thick outer lip. Horny operculum. COLOR: Exterior gray to reddish brown, sometimes with dark spiral stripes or mottling. Interior pinkish with four dark brown spots inside the outer lip.

HABITAT: Lives offshore. Common in offshore **Atlantic Calico Scallop** beds. Rarely washed onto ocean beaches. **RANGE:** Cape Hatteras to Brazil. **NOTES:** A carnivore, it uses radula and secretions to bore round holes into **Eastern Oyster** and other bivalve shells. Females lay ball-like masses of tongue-shaped egg capsules under rocks and on shells in early summer. Hatched young crawl away.

....

Florida Rocksnail
Stramonita floridana (Conrad, 1837)

DESCRIPTION: (3¾ inches) Medium-sized shell with a rough surface but without spines. Strong spiral lines. Sloped, sharply angled shoulders are sometimes knobby and sometimes nearly smooth (as pictured). Wide aperture with short, narrow upper canal and short, wide lower canal. Smooth inner lip. Thick, toothed outer lip. No parietal shield. Horny operculum. **COLOR:** Exterior gray to yellow with some brown spiral markings. Interior yellow orange to pink. **HABITAT:** Lives on rock jetties and oyster beds near inlets. Populous near Ocracoke. Occasionally found on ocean beaches. **RANGE:** Virginia to Brazil. **NOTES:** Also called a Southern Oyster Drill. A carnivore, it feeds on oysters and other mollusks. It is less of a threat to the oyster industry in North Carolina than in the Gulf of Mexico. Females lay funnel-shaped egg capsules. Young are free-swimming. When irritated, this mollusk can exude a poisonous, milky froth that turns purple. Its young, frequently confused with **Tinted Cantharus**, can be distinguished by color. See plate 36. **SCIENTIFIC NAME CHANGE:** Previous name, *Thais haemastoma floridana* (Conrad, 1837), is accepted to be a synonym for *Thais floridana*. The species has been reassigned to the genus *Stramonita*.

Florida Rocksnail

Atlantic Oyster Drill

Atlantic Oyster Drill
Urosalpinx cinerea (Say, 1822)

DESCRIPTION: (1½ inches) Rounded whorls with rough exterior; 9 to 12 large axial ribs, all equal in size, form a pattern of raised wavy lines. Less prominent spiral ridges cross the ribs. Rounded whorls. Wide aperture just less than half shell length, with a short, open lower canal. Smooth inner lip. Operculum. COLOR: Gray exterior, sometimes with light banding. Interior often violet or brownish. HABITAT: Lives in sounds and inlets, in and just below the intertidal zone. Commonly found living on pilings, rock jetties, and oyster reefs. Frequently found on sound and ocean beaches. RANGE: Nova Scotia, Canada, to Florida. NOTES: This species is a major oyster predator. Its effect on the North Carolina oyster industry is less devastating than in northern states. A carnivore, it actually prefers barnacles to oysters. It also feeds on other bivalves, gastropods, and crabs. It uses its radula to drill a tiny unbeveled hole through the shell and feed on the soft parts. Females lay rounded, funnel-shaped egg capsules on hard surfaces throughout the summer. Larval development and metamorphosis occur within encapsulated eggs and the young crawl away.

COSTELLARIIDAE (MITERS)

Generally small, slender-to-stout spindle-shaped shell; sharply pointed spire; narrow aperture; strong folds on inner aperture lip. Several species in North Carolina waters, mostly in deep water offshore and rarely found beached.

Waxy Miter

Waxy Miter

Vexillum wandoense (Holmes, 1859)

DESCRIPTION: (⅜ inch) Elongate spindle-shaped shell. Aperture less than half the total length. Numerous axial ribs crossed by incised lines, producing a very finely beaded surface. Three very strong toothlike folds on the columella. COLOR: Unavailable HABITAT: Commonly dredged in continental shelf waters, where it probably lives at depths of 30 to 100 feet; occasionally washed ashore in beach drift. RANGE: Cape Hatteras to Florida Keys, Gulf of Mexico, and the Caribbean.

OLIVIDAE (OLIVES)

Small to medium sized, cylindrical; long, narrow aperture extends almost the full length of shell; fresh shell quite glossy; animals active at night, crawling on sand with mantle covering top of shell; usually buried in daytime. Females produce translucent egg cases in sand; young hatch as veliger larvae.

Lettered Olive

Lettered Olive

Oliva sayana (Ravenel, 1834)

DESCRIPTION: (2½ inches) Smooth, shiny, cylindrical shell with a short spire. Narrow aperture extending almost length of shell, culminating in a short notch-shaped siphonal canal. Suture finely V-cut and deep. Lower part of whorl just above the suture extends outward and then at a sharp shoulder drops into the suture. No operculum. COLOR: Cream or grayish exterior with reddish-brown zigzag markings. HABITAT: Lives in near-shore waters just beyond the surf zone and on shallow sand flats near inlets. Commonly washed onto ocean beaches. RANGE: North Carolina to Gulf States. NOTES: This species is named for its dark surface markings that resemble letters. A carnivore, it captures bivalves and small crustaceans with its foot and takes them below the sand surface to digest. Its presence can sometimes be detected at very low tides by the trails it leaves when it crawls below the surface on semi-exposed sand flats. Females lay floating, round egg capsules that are often found in beach drift. Young are free-swimming. Early Native Americans and colonists made jewelry from these shells. See plate 37. SCIENTIFIC NAME CHANGE: Previously known as *Oliva sayana* (Ravenel, 1834).

....

Brown Olive

Brown Olive

Oliva nivosa clenchi (Petuch and Berschauer, 2019)

DESCRIPTION: (2½ inches) Very similar to the **Lettered Olive** except more robust, with (1) a shorter, less pointed spire, (2) a channel suture not deeply V-cut, and (3) a lower whorl portion that runs almost directly into the connecting suture. Also compare suture lines (see color notes). COLOR: Similar to Lettered Olive except (1) the pattern is lighter and more reticulated than zigzag; (2) the color is yellowish; and (3) brown spots run from the suture "thread" or "bleed" down the shell. HABITAT: Lives in deep offshore waters. Found by divers near shipwrecks; collected on sandy bottom near **Northern Lions-Paw Scallops** at 100-foot depth off Wrightsville Beach. Otherwise from Wrightsville Beach to just north of Cape Lookout, it seems restricted to the edge of the continental shelf at about 300-foot depths.

RANGE: Cape Lookout south at least to Florida. The other named subspecies of the *Oliva nivosa* species complex occur in Bermuda; southern Florida to the Dry Tortugas, a restricted region in the northeast Gulf of Mexico; and off the Yucatán coast and the Campeche Banks in Mexico. NOTES: The placement of this taxon is very confused in the literature. A very large number of species and subspecies names have been erected for western Atlantic (Caribbean) olives, and there is wide disagreement about synonymy and validity of names. SCIENTIFIC NAME CHANGE: In recent years the family Olividae has undergone extensive study and revision, including an updated name for this species. *Oliva bifasciata* (Weinkauff, 1878) is thought to now be restricted to the Caribbean.

....

Rice Olive

Rice Olive
Olivella floralia (Duclos, 1844)

DESCRIPTION: (⁷⁄₁₆ inch) Small, smooth, fusiform with a sharp apex. Columella with numerous, very small folds. Narrow, triangular aperture. Suture narrowly and deeply grooved. Spire a little more than half the total shell length. COLOR: Usually all white but often with a bluish undertone. Sometimes the body whorl is mottled brown. The apex can be white, orange, pink, or purplish. HABITAT: Lives in shallow high-salinity water on sandy bottoms. Commonly washed onto ocean beaches, readily found in high-tide drift lines. RANGE: North Carolina to Brazil. NOTES: Very common in tide line drift.

Variable Dwarf Olive

Variable Dwarf Olive

Olivella mutica (Say, 1822)

DESCRIPTION: (½ inch) Small, smooth, shiny, olive-shaped shell with rounded sides. Spire almost half the total shell length. Narrow, triangular aperture with a narrow upper canal and a wider lower canal. Inner aperture wall with a thickened callus that extends almost to the suture of the previous whorl. No operculum. COLOR: Highly variable, from uniformly creamy white to banded with up to three deep reddish-brown spiral bands. Occasionally solid brown. HABITAT: Lives on the sandy bottoms of sounds, inlets, and offshore areas. Common on sound and ocean beaches. RANGE: North Carolina to the Bahamas. NOTES: This species is a carnivore. Females lay dome-shaped egg capsules on hard surfaces. Hatched young crawl away. It is closely related to the **Lettered Olive**. Of the six possible *Olivella* species off the North Carolina coast, this one may be the most common in shallow water and easiest to identify. See plate 38.

CONIDAE (CONES)

Distinctly cone shaped, with nearly straight sides narrowing from the shoulder to the siphonal canal; narrow aperture extends most of length of shell; spire varies from nearly flat to about one-quarter the shell length. Cones have a venom gland and harpoon-shaped radular teeth, which they use to paralyze and capture their prey organisms, mostly worms and small mollusks. Live cones should be handled with some care; a few large tropical Pacific species immobilize and consume fish as prey, and their stings are known to have been fatal to humans.

Julia Cone

Julia Cone
Conus amphiurgus (Dall, 1889)

DESCRIPTION: (2 inches) Smooth, shiny, cone-shaped shell with a fairly high spire. Sides of whorls flattened. Body whorl sculptured by finely incised spiral lines and irregular growth lines. Slightly rounded shoulders. Narrow aperture almost length of shell. COLOR: Body whorl a light pinkish brown to orange with a creamy white spiral band at the middle. Middle band interrupted with axial bars of the body color, making it appear flecked with brown or broken spiral lines. Whitish spire with red streaks on the shoulder. HABITAT: Lives in deep offshore waters in rubble and sand. Collected by scuba divers on sandy bottom at 100-foot depths. RANGE: South of Cape Lookout to Texas and the Caribbean. NOTES: This species is rare. It has been found by divers. SCIENTIFIC NAME CHANGE: The original name, *Conus amphiurgus juliae* (Clench, 1942), is synonymous with *Conus amphiurgus* (Dall, 1889). Dall described the shell earlier, so his name takes precedence.

Largilliert's Cone

Largilliert's Cone
Conus largillierti (Kiener, 1845)

DESCRIPTION: (1½ inches) Smooth, shiny, cone-shaped shell. Fairly large spire with flat whorls. Narrow aperture almost the length of the shell. COLOR: Yellowish-orange shell with crowded dots. Body whorl with a whitish spiral band. Body is red in life. HABITAT: Lives offshore among **Atlantic Calico Scallop** beds. Rarely washed onto ocean beaches. RANGE: Cape Hatteras to southeastern Florida. NOTES: A carnivore that searches for prey at night. Females lay eggs in rows of flat capsules on hard surfaces or underneath rocks. Young probably undergo direct development without a free-swimming veliger stage. See plate 39. **SCIENTIFIC NAME CHANGE***:* Previously identified by Porter as *Conus floridanus f. floridensis* (Sowerby II, 1870), which is synonymous with *Conus anabathrum* (Crosse, 1865).

....

Agate Cone

Agate Cone
Conus ermineus (Born, 1778)

DESCRIPTION: (2½ inch) Shoulders rounded. Whorls slightly convex. Spire with four or five spiral threads on whorls. **COLOR:** Grayish white with brown, dark blue, or gray mottles. Thin periostracum. **HABITAT:** On shipwrecks and deep water reefs offshore. **RANGE:** Cape Hatteras to Florida, the Caribbean, and Brazil. **NOTES:** Uncommon. Not found on the beach.

....

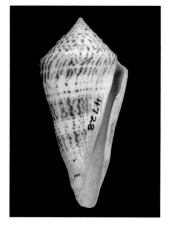

Sozon's Cone

Sozon's Cone
Conasprella delessertii (Récluz, 1843)

DESCRIPTION: (4 inches) Smooth, shiny, cone-shaped shell with a well-developed spire. Narrow aperture almost the length of the shell. Resembles the **Largilliert's Cone** but larger with different markings (see color notes). **COLOR:** Yellow orange with two wide white spiral bands. Many rows of irregular brown lines and spots encircle the shell. **HABITAT:** Lives offshore. Rarely found on ocean beaches. **RANGE:** North Carolina to Florida. **NOTES:** See Largilliert's Cone notes. This species was commonly brought in with **Atlantic Calico Scallop**

catches. See plate 40. **SCIENTIFIC NAME CHANGE:** Previous name: *Conus delessertii* (Récluz, 1843). The species has been reassigned to the genus *Conasprella*.

....

Stearn's Cone

Stearn's Cone

Conasprella stearnsii (Conrad, 1869)

DESCRIPTION: (¾ inch) Small, cone-shaped shell with a high spire that makes up about one-third the shell length. Sides of the spire form a 70-degree angle. Shoulders of early whorls concave with flat sides, making spire slightly concave. Body whorl sculptured with about 13 incised spiral lines. **COLOR:** Gray body whorl; brownish dots on incised spiral lines. **HABITAT:** Collected by scuba divers on sandy bottom at 65-foot depths. **RANGE:** South of Cape Lookout to Florida and Yucatán, Mexico. **NOTES:** Also widely known as Dusky Cone. *Conasprella pfleugeri* (Petuch, 2003), in southeast Florida, and originally named in the genus *Jaspidiconus*, may be a synonym for our North Carolina form. **SCIENTIFIC NAME CHANGE:** Previous name: *Conus stearnsii* (Conrad, 1869). The species has been reassigned to the genus *Conasprella*.

CLATHURELLIDAE (OXIAS)

This and the next three families discussed (Drilliidae, Mangeliidae, and Pseudomelatomidae) were long considered subfamilies of a very diverse group, collectively known as Turridae, "turrids," or "turret shells." On the basis of differences in structure of the radula and soft-part anatomical features and DNA, the Turridae have been divided into several families, not easily distinguished by shell characteristics. North Carolina representatives of these groups are all characterized by their small size, high spire, small aperture, and presence of a "turrid notch" in the outer aperture lip, near the top or rear of the aperture.

Smooth Oxia

Smooth Oxia
Nannodiella oxia (Bush, 1885)

DESCRIPTION: (³⁄₁₆ inch) Small, sharp, spindle-shaped shell with a high spire two-thirds the total shell length. Sharp nuclear whorl with at least three smooth translucent whorls and one whorl with a single raised spiral line. Crisscross appearance on each whorl caused at junctures where spiral and axial threads cross, creating sharp nodules. Spaces between the spiral and axial threads squarish and smooth to shiny. Beaded spiral lines on base of body whorl. Deep U-shaped turrid notch and moderately long lower canal on narrow aperture. Often the aperture's outer lip and bottom notch thicken into a large rib. COLOR: White to light pink. May have light pink spiral bands. HABITAT: Lives offshore at Cape Hatteras and south at depths of 100 feet and more. Known living on **Atlantic Calico Scallop** beds.

Occasionally washed onto ocean beaches. RANGE: North Carolina to Florida and Yucatán, Mexico. NOTES: This species is found in the stomach of the sea star *Astropecten articulatus*. See **White-Band Drillia** notes.

....

DRILLIIDAE (DRILLIAS)

See Clathurellidae family notes.

....

Simpson Drillia

Simpson Drillia

Lissodrillia simpsoni (Dall, 1887)

DESCRIPTION: (¼ inch) Small, spindle-shaped shell with a long, narrow spire about three-quarters the total shell length. About nine smooth, oily, axial ribs on each whorl. Axial ribs rounded, slightly S-shaped, and highest just above the lower whorl suture. Narrow aperture with a moderately deep turrid notch under the body whorl suture and a short lower canal. COLOR: Dead shells white to pink. Live specimens bright red. HABITAT: Has been found living south of Cape Hatteras near **Atlantic Calico Scallops**. RANGE: North Carolina to Gulf of Mexico. NOTES: Has been found in the stomach of the sea star *Astropecten articulatus*. See also **White-Band Drillia** notes. See plate 41. SCIENTIFIC NAME CHANGE: Previous name: *Cerodrillia simpsoni* (Dall, 1887). The species has been reassigned to the genus *Lissodrillia*.

Glorious Drillia

....

Glorious Drillia
Neodrillia cydia (Bartsch, 1843)

DESCRIPTION: (½ inch) Spindle-shaped shell with a long, narrow spire about two-thirds the total shell length. Whorls with six to nine distinct axial ribs that are blunt to rounded. Distinct, crowded spiral lines cross axial ribs and spaces between the ribs. Two and a half smooth whorls on nuclear whorl. Narrow aperture with a deep, almost tubular turrid notch just under the body whorl suture and an open lower canal. COLOR: White. Sometimes a row of brown spots at the base of the axial ribs. HABITAT: Known offshore of Cape Lookout and Cape Fear at 70-to-300-foot depths. Has been collected from **Atlantic Calico Scallop** beds and by scuba divers on sandy bottom at 80-foot depths off Wrightsville Beach. RANGE: South of Cape Lookout to Florida and the Caribbean. NOTES: Its feeding technique is similar to that of the **White-Band Drillia** except its prey are sipunculid worms. SCIENTIFIC NAME CHANGE: Previous name: *Drillia cydia* (Bartsch, 1943). The species has been reassigned to the genus *Neodrillia*.

MANGELIIDAE (MANGELIAS)

See Clathurellidae family notes.

....

Waxy Mangelia
Cryoturris cerinella (Dall, 1889)

DESCRIPTION: (¼ inch) Small, narrow, spindle-shaped shell with a spire two-thirds the total shell length. Whorl of fine axial riblets following two smooth, rounded nuclear whorls. Seven to nine

Waxy Mangelia

moderately sized and obtusely angled axial ribs on each whorl. These ribs are crossed by crowded microscopically beaded spiral lines. Several stronger, threadlike spiral lines on each whorl. Narrow aperture with a shallow turrid notch and a short lower canal. COLOR: Yellowish white. Crowded, microscopically beaded spiral lines that make the whorl surface appear frosted. HABITAT: Found living south of Cape Lookout at 30-to-70-foot depths. Occasionally washed onto ocean beaches south of Cape Lookout. Also found on **Atlantic Calico Scallop** beds. RANGE: North Carolina to Florida and Texas. NOTES: This species is difficult to distinguish from other small turrids in North Carolina waters, such as the Fargo's Mangelia (*Cryoturris fargoi* [McGinty, 1955]) and the Punctate Mangelia (*Kurtziella limonitella* [Dall, 1884]). It has been found in the stomach of the sea star *Astropecten articulatus*. See **White-Band Drillia** notes for feeding method.

....

Plicate Mangelia
Pyrgocythara plicosa (C. B. Adams, 1850)

Plicate Mangelia

DESCRIPTION: (¼ inch) Small, stubby, spindle-shaped shell. About nine strong, rounded axial ribs crossed by three to four slightly weaker spiral ribs—a pattern then continues on the body whorl to the upper aperture canal. U-shaped, moderately deep turrid notch on narrow aperture. Often, the aperture's outer lip and the upper notch thicken into a large rib. Aperture length about equal to the shell width and slightly less than half the total shell length. COLOR: White to reddish brown. HABITAT: Lives in moderate-to-high-salinity estuaries, often associated with eelgrass beds and oyster beds. Rarely found offshore. Occasionally washed onto ocean and sound beaches. **RANGE:** Cape Cod, Massachusetts, to Florida and Texas. **NOTES:** Also called a Plicate Turret Shell. See **White-Band Drillia** notes.

....

Reddish Mangelia

Reddish Mangelia

Rubellatoma rubella (Kurtz and W. Stimpson, 1851)

DESCRIPTION: (⅜ inch) Spindle-shaped shell with a moderately high spire just more than half the total shell length. Shell's width about one-third its length. Two smooth nuclear whorls. Eight to nine obtusely angled, slightly S-shaped axial ribs on the surface that are covered by crowded microscopic spiral threads. Axial ribs extend from body whorl to just above the aperture's lower canal. Long, narrow aperture with a shallow turrid notch and a somewhat lengthened lower canal. **COLOR:** Grayish cream with a wide spiral band of light to dark red just below the whorl suture. Several similar bands below shoulder on body whorl. **HABITAT:** Lives offshore to depths of 50 feet or more. Has been found on **Atlantic Calico Scallop** beds. Occasionally washed onto ocean beaches south of Cape Hatteras. **RANGE:** North Carolina to Florida and Texas. **NOTES:** This species may be found in the stomach of the sea star *Astropecten articulatus.* See **White-Band Drillia** notes. **SCIENTIFIC NAME CHANGE:** Previous name: *Kurtziella rubella* (Kurtz and W. Stimpson, 1851). The species has been reassigned to the genus *Rubellatoma.*

....

PSEUDOMELATOMIDAE (DRILLIAS)

See Clathurellidae family notes.

White-Band Drillia

White-Band Drillia

Pilsbryspira albomaculata (d'Orbigny, 1842)

DESCRIPTION: (⅜ inch) Chunky, spindle-shaped shell with a spire about two-thirds the total shell length. About two spiral cords on each whorl— lower cord larger and knobbed. Spiral cords reach from shoulder of the body whorl to upper canal of the narrow aperture. Deep, almost closed, tubular notch at upper end of aperture (turrid notch). **COLOR:** Dark brown shell with a whitish or yellowish band (following the knobbed spiral cord). **HABITAT:** Known in North Carolina waters at depths of 35 to 55 feet. Found by scuba divers with **Northern Lions-Paw Scallops** in the offshore Cape Fear area. Rare on ocean beaches. **RANGE:** Cape Lookout to Florida, Texas, and the Caribbean. **NOTES:** All members of turrid families, like cone shells, have a radula with venomous dart-like teeth. These teeth are not known to be venomous to humans but are used on the animal's prey— generally polychaete worms.

TEREBRIDAE (AUGERS)

Like the cones and the turrids, most augers possess a venom gland and associated radulae, which they use to narcotize and capture prey. Shell characterized by extremely high, sharply pointed spire; small squarish aperture; and short, well-defined siphonal canal. Larval metamorphosis occurs within the egg capsules, and the hatched young crawl away.

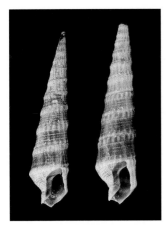

Concave Auger

Concave Auger
Neoterebra concava (Say, 1826)

DESCRIPTION: (1 inch) Long, slender spire. Similar to **Eastern Auger** except shorter and proportionately narrower and the whorls have concave sides. Beaded spiral rows. Twisted canal at bottom of aperture. Thin operculum. **COLOR:** Yellowish-gray exterior. Tan operculum. **HABITAT:** Lives offshore and in high-salinity estuaries; occasionally washed onto ocean beaches. **RANGE:** North Carolina to Brazil. **NOTES:** Hatched young crawl away. **SCIENTIFIC NAME CHANGE:** Previous name: *Terebra concava* (Say, 1826). The species has been reassigned to the genus *Neoterebra*.

Eastern Auger

Eastern Auger
Neoterebra dislocata (Say, 1822)

DESCRIPTION: (2¼ inches) Long, pointed spire. Whorls not concave. Prominent spiral cord at top of each whorl that winds around 20 to 25 low axial ribs. Smaller spiral cords between axial ribs. Canal at bottom of aperture. Thin operculum. **COLOR:** Varied exterior with bands of pale gray, pinkish brown, or orange brown. Tan operculum. **HABITAT:** Lives in sounds on shallow and intertidal sand flats and offshore. Common on sound and ocean beaches. **RANGE:** Virginia to Brazil. **NOTES:** Also called a Common American Auger or Atlantic Auger. A carnivore, it lacks the radula and venom gland found in most other augers. Hatched young crawl away. **SCIENTIFIC NAME CHANGE:** Previous name: *Terebra dislocata* (Say, 1822). The species has been reassigned to the genus *Neoterebra*. See plate 42.

ARCHITECTONICIDAE (SUNDIALS)

Medium-sized top-shaped shell; flattened; large, deep, crenulated umbilicus. At least five species in North Carolina: all live well offshore and, except for one, are rarely seen. Shell width is greater than shell height. Sundials feed on the polyps of corals and other coelenterates and cnidarians.

Common Sundial

Common Sundial

Architectonica nobilis (Röding, 1798)

DESCRIPTION: (2¼ inches wide) Round, broad shell; top shaped with a very flat base. Prominent beaded spiral cords on top and bottom. Rounded or elliptical aperture. Deep, crenulated, funnel-shaped hole (umbilicus) in base of shell. Horny operculum. COLOR: Whitish exterior with spiral rows of brown spots. Brown operculum. HABITAT: Lives offshore south of Cape Hatteras (particularly between Cape Hatteras and Cape Lookout). Rarely found on ocean beaches. RANGE: North Carolina to Brazil. NOTES: Has been found in association with the cnidarian sea pansy (*Renilla reniformis*), on which it probably feeds. Its long, free-swimming larval stage results in wide dispersal.

BULLIDAE (BUBBLES)

Oval to cylindrical; aperture extending length of shell; globular lower end of aperture wider than upper end.

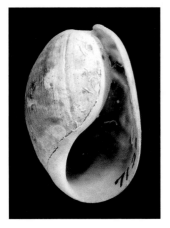

Striate Bubble

....

Striate Bubble
Bulla striata (Bruguière, 1792)

DESCRIPTION: (1¾ inches wide) Smooth, shiny, oval shell; looks as though rolled up or folded over. Spire deeply hidden in a depression at the apex. Aperture extends length of the shell, narrow above and much wider and rounded below. Columella smoothly rounded into outer lip. No siphonal canal. No operculum. **COLOR:** Mottled light and dark brown exterior. **HABITAT:** Occasionally found washed onto ocean beaches. **RANGE:** North Carolina to Brazil. **NOTES:** Also called a Common Atlantic Bubble. An omnivore, it feeds on other mollusks and algae at night. It burrows just below sand surface during the day. This species is a hermaphrodite. *Bulla occidentalis* (A. Adams, 1850) is a more southern species.

TORNATINIDAE (BARREL-BUBBLES)

Very small, cylindrical; narrow aperture almost the length of shell; tiny spire (the protoconch) protrudes above apex; a folded ridge encircles the columella; no siphonal canal.

Channeled Barrel-Bubble

....

Channeled Barrel-Bubble
Acteocina canaliculata (Say, 1826)

DESCRIPTION: (less than ¼ inch) Similar to **Candé Barrel-Bubble** except early whorls almost completely submerged in the spire. Shoulder suture slightly channeled and without a spiral carina. **COLOR:** White to cream with rust-like staining. **HABITAT:** Lives in estuarine waters. Found in beach drift. **RANGE:** Nova Scotia, Canada, to Florida,

Texas, and the Caribbean. **NOTES:** Females lay eggs in a round jellylike mass that is attached by a stalk to the sand or mud. Larvae either develop immediately into crawling young or pass through a short free-swimming stage.

....

Candé Barrel-Bubble

Candé Barrel-Bubble

Acteocina candei (d'Orbigny, 1841)

DESCRIPTION: (less than ¼ inch) Very small, smooth, glossy shell. Barrel- to spindle-shaped with straightish sides. Short spire with early whorls at 90-degree angle to later whorls (heterotopic condition). Spiral carina on the shoulder suture. Narrow aperture almost the length of shell, widening out at the front end. Columella with a thickened fold. **COLOR:** Milky white. **HABITAT:** Lives in high-salinity estuaries and just offshore. Found in beach drift south of Cape Hatteras. **RANGE:** North Carolina to Argentina. **NOTES:** Larvae are free-swimming.

....

PYRAMIDELLIDAE (PYRAMS, ODOSTOMES)

A large group of very small gastropods, many of them very similar in general appearance. Most are parasitic on other mollusks and various other organisms. Most pyramidellids have a very high spire, bluntly pointed, and small oval/round aperture with no notable siphonal canal.

....

Impressed Odostome

Boonea impressa (Say, 1822)

DESCRIPTION: (¼ inch) Very small shell with a high spire. Three or four strong spiral cords on each of the six or seven whorls. Oval aperture about one-third the length of the shell. COLOR: Milky white. HABITAT: Lives in estuaries, often feeding on **Eastern Oysters**. Occasionally found on sound and ocean beaches. RANGE: Massachusetts to Florida and Gulf of Mexico. NOTES: A parasite, it uses its proboscis and spine to feed on the mantle tissue of oysters when their valves are slightly open. If too many are feeding on one oyster, the oyster's condition can become weakened. This species also may feed on sea squirts (tunicates).

Impressed Odostome

....

Half-Smooth Odostome

Boonea seminuda (C. B. Adams, 1839)

DESCRIPTION: (less than ¼ inch) Very small shell with a high spire. Four to six strong spiral cords on whorls crossed by equally strong axial ribs, creating a waffled appearance. Only the spiral cords are strong on the whorl base. Oval aperture almost half the length of the shell. COLOR: White. HABITAT: Lives in estuaries and offshore waters. Occasionally found on sound and ocean beaches. RANGE: Nova Scotia, Canada, to Florida and Texas. NOTES: A parasite, it uses a piercing spine and long proboscis to suck up fluids and soft tissue at the valve edges of **Bay Scallops** and **Atlantic Calico Scallops**. When a scallop's valves are slightly open, the snail will feed on its mantle tissue. It also may feed on slippersnails.

Half-Smooth Odostome

Crenulated Pyram

Crenulated Pyram
Longchaeus suturalis (H. C. Lea, 1843)

DESCRIPTION: (½ inch) Slender, conical shell with a spire about three to four times the aperture length. About 12 smooth, flat whorls with deeply channeled sutures. Body whorl slightly angular at one end. Oval aperture. Horny operculum. COLOR: Cream with tan blotches. HABITAT: Lives in high-salinity estuaries and on offshore sandy bottoms. Can be commonly found washed onto beaches south of Cape Hatteras. RANGE: North Carolina to Florida and Texas. NOTES: A parasite, it uses its proboscis and spine to feed on soft tissues of mollusks and other marine animals.

ELLOBIIDAE (MELAMPI)

Semiterrestrial gastropods, living at or near the high-tide line in estuarine areas, usually at the edge of salt marshes (in *Spartina* and *Juncus*). Small, robust, fat shell; cone-shaped spire; folds on the lower columella; tan to dark brown in color.

Eastern Melampus

Eastern Melampus
Melampus bidentatus (Say, 1822)

DESCRIPTION: (⅝ inch) Small, cone-shaped shell with a short, blunt spire. Sides of the spire form a 90-degree angle. Fine spiral lines on spire and body whorl. Long, narrow aperture with front end expanded. About nine spiral ridges on outer lip; two to three folds on inner lip. COLOR: Light to dark brown, occasionally with three to four darker brown spiral bands. HABITAT: Lives in the high-tide zone of salt marshes in moderate-to-high-salinity estuaries. Typically found under boards or marsh grass (*Spartina*) litter or at the base of *Spartina* stalks. Occasionally found on some sound beaches. **RANGE:** Nova Scotia, Canada, to Texas and the Caribbean. **NOTES:** Also called a Salt-Marsh Snail. This family has a primitive lung in place of gills and breathes air. The snail eats decaying plant matter but is believed to get its nutrients from the bacteria that live on decaying matter. Female lays eggs in jellylike mounds, each containing about 840 eggs. Larvae settle to the bottom during autumn's spring tides (high tides during full and new moons).

....

Florida Melampus

Florida Melampus
Melampus floridanus (L. Pfeiffer, 1856)

DESCRIPTION: (less than ¼ inch) Similar to the **Eastern Melampus** except smaller with a higher spire and no incised spiral lines on the shoulder. About 10 spiral ridges on outer lip. One large and one small tooth or ridge on inner lip. **COLOR:** Glossy dark brown with several light brown spiral bands on the body whorl. **HABITAT:** Lives on or under marsh debris in the high-tide zone of low-salinity marshes, sometimes alongside the Eastern Melampus. **RANGE:** New Jersey to Louisiana. **NOTES:** Large colonies of this species may be found living in a restricted area. Like the Eastern Melampus, it breathes air with primitive lungs. Its feeding habits also may be similar. Females lay 20 to 50 eggs in dome-like, gelatinous masses. Free-swimming larvae hatch in about two weeks. Crabs, fish, and birds prey on the adults. **SCIENTIFIC NAME CHANGE:** Previous name: *Detracia floridana* (L. Pfeiffer, 1856). The species has been reassigned to the genus *Melampus*.

Species
Descriptions
More Mollusks

....

THE FOLLOWING CLASSES AND FAMILIES are arranged in alphabetical order.

Cephalopoda
    Argonautidae
    Spirulidae

Polyplacophora
    Chaetopleuridae
    Ischnochitonidae

Scaphopoda
    Dentaliidae
    Gadilidae

Cephalopoda by Family

ARGONAUTIDAE (ARGONAUTS)

A family of (six to eight, globally) cephalopod species closely related to octopuses but adapted to a free-swimming pelagic existence in warm tropical waters. Female argonauts produce a thin, fragile shell called a paper nautilus, in which they carry and brood their eggs. The shell is produced not by their mantles but by two specialized flap-like tentacles that are absent in much smaller males. The female argonaut envelops and holds on to her egg case with those tentacles, nestles into the paper nautilus, and maintains her buoyancy by releasing gas bubbles into the shell. It receives one or more packets of sperm from a tiny male argonaut and then carries fertilized eggs until they hatch into fully developed young, after which the female dies. Only one species is known in North Carolina's Gulf Stream waters.

Greater Argonaut

Greater Argonaut
Argonauta argo (Linnaeus, 1758)

DESCRIPTION: (8 inches) Thin, fragile paper nautilus shell, with a narrow keel and numerous sharp nodules. COLOR: Milky white stained with dark purple brown. HABITAT: Pelagic. May be found in stomachs of large Gulf Stream fish popular with anglers. Very rarely washed ashore on beach. RANGE: Tropical waters worldwide. NOTES: See plate 43.

SPIRULIDAE (SPIRULAS)

Fragile, coiled internal shell with chambers that the living animal uses to control buoyancy.

Ram's Horn Squid

Ram's Horn Squid

Spirula spirula (Linnaeus, 1758)

DESCRIPTION: (1 inch) Flat, fragile, loosely coiled shell resembling a ram's horn. Interior partitioned into chambers. COLOR: Pure white exterior and interior. HABITAT: Pelagic, lives offshore in the Gulf Stream. Occasionally washed onto ocean beaches, especially after storms. RANGE: Worldwide. NOTES: Also called a Common Spirula. This internal shell is produced by a living deep-sea squid. Its inner chambers are filled with gas, causing the shell to float when the animal dies.

Polyplacophora by Family

CHAETOPLEURIDAE (CHITONS)

Bilaterally symmetrical mollusks, with elongate, oval bodies covered by eight shell plates, articulated with each other and surrounded by a leathery girdle. They live attached to, and crawling on, hard surfaces such as rocks. Found from the intertidal areas to shallow offshore waters. Shaped somewhat like limpets, their forward-facing mouth is equipped with a radula used in grazing algae. Very few species in North Carolina, not commonly found washed onto beaches. Families are distinguished by anatomical differences and by details in the articulation of the plates.

Eastern Beaded Chiton

Eastern Beaded Chiton

Chaetopleura apiculata (Say, 1834)

DESCRIPTION: (1 inch) Flattened oval mollusk covered by eight articulated shelly valves, or plates, encircled by a girdle. Valves angled toward the center and have up to 20 longitudinal rows of raised beads. Girdle beaded with scattered, short, microscopic hairs. COLOR: Light gray, sometimes reddish. HABITAT: Lives attached to shells in subtidal shelly areas of high-salinity estuaries near inlets and just offshore. Rarely seen on ocean beaches. RANGE: Massachusetts to Florida. NOTES: Also called the Common Eastern Chiton. A flattened foot attaches the chiton to hard substrates.

ISCHNOCHITONIDAE (CHITONS).

See Chaetopleuridae family notes.

Striolate Chiton

Striolate Chiton
Ischnochiton striolatus (Gray, 1828)

DESCRIPTION: (½ inch) Similar to **Eastern Beaded Chiton** except smaller. Differs from young Eastern Beaded Chiton in having randomly placed beads on its outer surface, not longitudinal rows of raised beads. Also in this species, the girdle is covered with overlaying scales; the surface is not grainy with short hairs as found in the Eastern Beaded Chiton. COLOR: Whitish, mottled with greenish brown. HABITAT: Lives in mouth of inlets on shelly bottoms. Known in intertidal area of Beaufort Inlet and in Cape Lookout Bight. RANGE: North Carolina, lower Florida, and the Caribbean. NOTES: Also called a Mesh-Pitted Chiton.

Scaphopoda by Family

DENTALIIDAE (TUSKSHELLS)

Strongly resembles an elephant's tusk, with a long, slightly curved shell, open at both the small (apex) and the large (aperture) ends. The animals live partially buried in soft, sandy sediments and feed, using specialized tentacles, on microscopic organisms such as foraminifera. Reproduction is by random broadcast of eggs and sperm, external fertilization, and larval development through free-swimming trochophore and veliger larval stages. Several species are in North Carolina, most of them in deep water off the continental shelf.

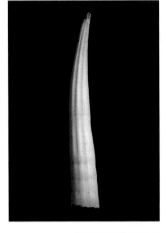

Reticulate Tuskshell

Reticulate Tuskshell
Dentalium laqueatum (A. E. Verrill, 1885)

DESCRIPTION: (2 inches) Small, hollow, tusklike shell with 9 to 12 strong ribs running the length of the shell but fading toward the apex. Concave spaces between ribs. Curved apex. COLOR: Dull white. HABITAT: Lives in deep offshore waters (200 to 750 feet deep). RANGE: North Carolina to Brazil. NOTES: This is North Carolina's largest and heaviest tuskshell. Rarely washes ashore. See also **Ivory Tuskshell** notes.

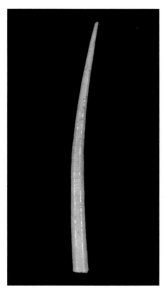

. . . .

Ivory Tuskshell

Graptacme eborea (Conrad, 1846)

DESCRIPTION: (2 inches) Small, hollow shell. Shiny, slender, and slightly curved like an elephant's tusk. A deep, narrow, fragile apical slit on convex side. **COLOR:** Glossy white to pinkish. **HABITAT:** Lives buried in mud or sand in deep water. Very commonly washed onto ocean beaches, most often found in the high- or low-tide drift lines. **RANGE:** North Carolina to Brazil. **NOTES:** Only the narrow end of the shell protrudes from the mud. A carnivore, it uses its lobed appendages to capture tiny bivalves and other organisms. Eggs and sperm are released into the water, and fertilization takes place there. Young are free-swimming. Water enters and waste leaves through a hole in the aboveground part of the shell. Twenty-four kinds of tuskshells have been recorded off the North Carolina coast; most of them are small, difficult to identify, and from deep water.

Ivory Tuskshell

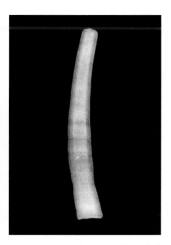

. . . .

American Tuskshell

Paradentalium americanum (Chenu, 1843)

DESCRIPTION: (1 inch) Hollow, tusklike shell. Slender, curved, and hexagonal in cross section. Six ribs running the length of the shell. Flat, broad spaces between ribs. **COLOR:** Dull, grayish white. **HABITAT:** Lives buried in mud or sand in deep water. Occasionally washed up in the high- or low-tide drift lines of sound or ocean beaches. **RANGE:** North Carolina to Brazil. **NOTES:** Also called a Texas Tusk. See family notes. **SCIENTIFIC NAME CHANGE:** Previous name: *Dentalium americanum* (Chenu, 1843). The species has been reassigned to the genus *Paradentalium*.

American Tuskshell

GADILIDAE (TOOTHSHELLS)

Similar to tuskshells but significantly smaller. Shell is sculptureless, smooth, polished; slender with a distinct curve and may have a swollen middle. Open at both ends. The aperture is always smaller than the widest section of the shell and usually has 4 slits. They generally inhabit deeper water and burrow into soft sediments. They are deposit feeders, obtaining nutrition from organic matter in the sediment.

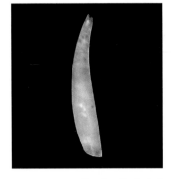

Carolina Toothshell

Carolina Toothshell
Polyschides carolinensis (K. J. Bush, 1885)

DESCRIPTION: (½ to ⅜ inch) Small, tusk-shaped shell. Slightly swollen below center. Apex with four shallow slits. **COLOR:** White. **HABITAT:** In sand, from depths of 50 to 300 feet. **RANGE:** North Carolina to Texas. **NOTES:** Very commonly found in beach drift.

Glossary

accessory plates: Small, shelly plates over the hinge of some bivalves, such as in Pholadidae.

adductor muscles: The muscles (usually two, sometimes only one) that tightly close a bivalve's shell.

algae: A diverse group of nonvascular photosynthetic aquatic plants, including many species fed upon by mollusks; see also **phytoplankton**.

anoxic: Lacking oxygen.

aperture: Opening in a gastropod shell through which the mollusk's body extends.

apex: The pointed tip of a gastropod shell where shell growth began.

axial ribs: Lengthwise (not spiral) ridgelike sculptural features on a gastropod shell.

ballast water: Fresh- or saltwater carried in the cargo holds of ships, which can be a major source of introduction for invasive marine species into ecosystems.

beak: The pointed part near the hinge of bivalve shells where larval shell growth began, or for octopuses, the small jaws located in the center of the arms.

bivalve: Mollusk with paired shells (e.g., clams, oysters, mussels) connected by a hinge.

body whorl: Most recent, and usually largest, 360-degree revolution of shell growth in a gastropod.

byssus: Threads produced by some bivalves (e.g., Mytilidae, Pinnidae) for attaching themselves to rocks or other substrates.

callus: Thickened calcareous section of shell, usually at the gastropod aperture opposite the outer lip.

cardinal teeth: Interlocking teeth just beneath the beak in a bivalve hinge.

carina: Keel-like sculptural feature on shell surface.

carnivore: Animal that feeds on other animals.

cephalopod: A class of mollusks that include the squids, cuttlefish, and octopuses.

chevron-shaped: V-shaped, as a color pattern or sculptural feature.

chiton: The common name for the Polyplacophora class of mollusks with eight articulated shelly plates within a leathery girdle.

class: A taxon below phylum and above order.

columella: The central twisted "core" or axis of the gastropod shell around which the animal winds its whorls during growth; visible externally only at the base of the inner aperture and siphonal canal, the columella is often reinforced with ridges.

concentric: Occurring in a growing succession of arcs or circles, as in the sculptural features around the beaks of a bivalve.

conchiolin: Collective term for the structural proteins incorporated into mollusk shells during growth.

coral: Colonial reef-forming marine animals of the phylum Cnidaria (along with jellyfish and sea anemones).

costae: Riblike axial flanges, sometimes thin and fragile, marking former varices on some gastropod shells.

crenulations: A finely notched or wavy pattern usually at the edge of a shell.

deposit feeder: An animal that feeds on or at the surface layer of soft sediment.

detritivore: An animal that feeds on dead and decaying materials (detritus).

detritus: Dead and decaying particulate material, primarily organic, that settles from the water column to the bottom sediments.

dextral: The usual direction of coiling exhibited in most marine gastropod species (clockwise looking down at the spire); also known as right-handed. See also **sinistral**.

DNA (deoxyribonucleic acid): A double-stranded, helical, replicating molecule that is present in all living organisms and carries their genetic information.

ears: In seashells, the flat extensions on either side of the beak and hinge of a bivalve (especially in scallops).

echinoderm: A member of the phylum Echinodermata; marine animals often with stiff, spiny shells and an endoskeleton made of ossicles (sea urchins, sea stars, sea cucumbers).

estuary: Coastal water body where ocean water mixes with freshwater that drains from land.

family: A taxonomic rank in the classification of organisms, between genus and order.

flammule: A flame-like pattern or streak of color in a shell.

gastropod: A member of the class of mollusks with a single, usually spirally coiled shell or, in some cases (slugs and nudibranchs), without a visible shell as an adult.

genus: A taxonomic category ranking used in biological classification, below family and above species.

girdle: The muscular, leathery band surrounding the eight shell plates of a chiton.

growth lines: A succession of lines (sometimes annual) representing prior shell edges; may be visible on the surface of a shell.

herbivore: An animal that feeds on plants.

hermaphrodite: An animal that has both male and female sex organs, either simultaneously or sequentially.

heterodont: Bivalve hinge type with cardinal teeth and lateral teeth.

hinge: In seashells, the area where the two bivalve shells articulate with a ligament and teeth.

inflated: Enlarged or swollen, as a portion of a shell.

intertidal zone: The zone between low tide and high tide along a shoreline.

iridescent: Pearly and showing luminous changing color in different light, as a shell surface.

isodont: A bivalve hinge dentition consisting of a small number of hinge teeth and sockets, positioned symmetrically on both sides of a resilient ligament; for example, in many Plicatulidae and Spondylidae.

jetties: Structures, usually rock, built to alter currents and slow erosion on shorelines.

larva: Early stage of molluscan development, after hatching either from an egg (indirect) or sometimes within the egg itself (direct).

lateral teeth: The usually longer teeth (in front of and behind the cardinal teeth) in a bivalve hinge.

ligament: The elastic cartilage-like structure that (1) binds the two shells of a bivalve together and (2) opens the shells when the bivalve relaxes its adductor muscles.

lips: The inner and outer peripheries of the aperture (edge of the body whorl) in a gastropod shell.

lunule: Incised depression in front of the beaks of a bivalve shell; a half-heart shape in each valve.

mantle: The delicate fleshy tissue that encompasses the soft parts of the mollusk and at its edge secretes the shell materials and pigments during shell growth; also involved in respiration.

muscle scars: Circular features, usually depressed, where the adductor muscles were attached to the inside of a bivalve shell.

nacreous: Shiny and iridescent, as in a layer of shell (from "nacre," or mother-of-pearl).

nuclear whorls: The first tiny whorls at the tip of a gastropod shell, formed during the larval stage.

omnivore: An animal that feeds on both plants and animals.

operculum: A structure on the top of the foot of some gastropods that partially or completely closes the aperture when the animal is retracted; sometimes called the trapdoor; calcified and hard in some species.

pallial line: Incised line, useful in bivalve identification, that runs inside the shell edge between the muscle scars of a bivalve shell, indicating where the mantle edge rests while the valves are closed.

pallial sinus: A fold in the posterior part of the pallial line marking where the bivalve's siphons lay at rest (shallow pallial sinus indicates short siphons in shallow-burrowing bivalves; large, deep sinus indicates long siphons and deep burrowing).

parietal shield: A broadly thickened flat section of callus on the inner lip, especially prominent in the helmet shells (Cassidae).

periostracum: The outer skin-like covering on a live mollusk shell.

phylum: A major taxonomic rank below kingdom.

phytoplankton: The diverse community of photosynthetic plants, mostly microscopic, single-celled diatoms and blue-green algae, that live in the surface waters (where sunlight penetrates) of the ocean; they serve as the base of the food chain for the dependent zooplankton and nekton elements of aquatic life.

plankton: The portion of the living aquatic community that drifts with the water mass; that is, plants and animals incapable of maintaining their positions (swimming) against prevailing currents; see also **phytoplankton** and **zooplankton**.

proboscis: A tubelike extension of a gastropod's head bearing the radula internally and the mouth at the tip.

protoconch: The portion of a gastropod shell grown during larval development; located at the apex of the shell, it consists of one to five nuclear whorls.

radial: Describing the sculptural pattern of a bivalve and the features (lines, ridges) that radiate from the beak to the edge of the shell.

radula: Ribbonlike structure of teeth in the proboscis of gastropods used in feeding (and drilling holes in shells of prey); often used by experts in identification.

salinity: Measure of saltiness in water, with seawater having higher salinity than freshwater.

scaphopod: A marine mollusk of the class Scaphopoda, including tusk- and tooth-shaped shells.

scavenger: An animal that feeds on dead and decaying plants and animals.

sculpture: The three-dimensional structural ornamentation on the surface of a mollusk shell, including ribs, ridges, grooves, and spiral lines.

shell hash: A sedimentary type composed of shells that have become granulated over time, often serving as habitat for living mollusks.

shoulder: Sharp angular edge of the whorl of a gastropod shell, most frequently just below the suture.

sinistral: Gastropod shells coiled counterclockwise when looking down on the spire; left-handed; a rare mutation in most marine species but the normal form for the Lightning Whelk; opposite of **dextral**.

siphon: In a bivalve, tubelike extension at the rear of the mantle through which the animal draws water, oxygen, and food and expels wastes; in a gastropod, the siphon is in front and used for transporting respiratory gases and aiding chemoreception.

siphonal canal: The opening at the base or front of some gastropod apertures where the siphon protrudes even when the body is retracted into the shell; lacking or greatly reduced in many species.

species: A group of closely related organisms that can produce viable offspring.

spiral ribs: Ribs, ridges, or other structural features arranged in a spiral pattern around a gastropod shell.

spire: The whorl above the body whorl (to the tip) of a gastropod shell.

stromboid notch: Unique characteristic of the family Strombidae; a shallow notch at the front of the outer lip edge and near the siphonal canal, affording protection for the conch's right eye.

suspension feeder: A bivalve that feeds on food particles suspended in the water.

suture: The juncture between successive whorls in a gastropod shell, usually just above the shoulder.

taxodont: A specialized arrangement of bivalve hinge teeth where many small teeth are tightly aligned in a relatively straight transverse row across the hinge, most notably in Arcidae and Glycymerididae.

trochophore: The larval form of marine annelids and most groups of mollusks.

truncate: A shell margin that appears shortened or sharply and squarely cut off.

turrid notch: A characteristic notch in the upper outer lip of many members of the gastropod family Turridae.

umbilicus: The funnel-like opening in the base of some gastropod shells, surrounded by the columella and interior walls of the successive whorls; varies from widely open (e.g., in sundials) to narrow (in Northern Moonsnail) and nearly closed or absent (in olives and cones) in very tightly coiled shells; see also **columella**.

umbo: The oldest part of a bivalve shell, generally rounded and located where the two valves are attached; also known as the beak.

valve: One of the two paired shells of a bivalve.

varix: Each of the prominent ridges on the shell of a gastropod mollusk, marking an earlier position of the aperture and outer lip.

veliger: The final planktonic larval stage of bivalves, scaphopods, and many (more primitive) gastropod families.

wampum: Shell beads carved and woven into belts and used as money by Native Americans.

whorl: Each full revolution of a gastropod shell, from nuclear whorl to body whorl.

zooplankton: The animal elements of the drifting planktonic community, including microscopic protozoans, larvae of echinoderms, mollusks, crustaceans, and fish, along with larger jellyfish and some small adult crustacea (krill) and fish.

References and Recommended Resources

REFERENCES

This listing includes older publications that may not have current names, taxonomy, and classifications. They have, however, contributed to the progression of science on this topic through the decades, including that presented in earlier editions from North Carolina Sea Grant.

Abbott, R. T. 1954. *American Seashells*. New York: Van Nostrand.
———. 1974. *American Seashells*. 2nd ed. New York: Van Nostrand Reinhold.
———. 1986. *Seashells of North America: A Guide to Field Identification*. A Golden Guide. New York: St. Martin's. Newer editions are also available.
Abbott, R. T., and P. A. Morris. 2001. *Field Guide to Shells of the Atlantic and Gulf Coasts and the West Indies*. 4th ed. Boston: Houghton Mifflin.
Bergeron, E. 1973. *How to Clean Seashells*. Rev. ed. St. Petersburg, FL: Great Outdoors.
Bouchet, P., J. Rocroi, R. Bieler, J. G. Carter, and E. V. Coan. 2010. "Nomenclator of Bivalve Families with a Classification of Bivalve Families." *Malacologia* 52 (2):1–184.
Bouchet, P., J. Rocroi, B. Hausdorf, A. Kaim, Y. Kano, A. Nützel, P. Parkhaev, M. Schrödl, and E. E. Strong. 2017. "Revised Classification, Nomenclator and Typification of Gastropod and Monoplacophoran Families." *Malacologia* 61 (1–2):1–526.
Carson, R. 1951. *The Sea around Us*. New York: Oxford University Press.
———. 1955. *The Edge of the Sea*. Boston: Houghton Mifflin.
———. 1962. *Silent Spring*. Boston: Houghton Mifflin.
Chandler, R. E., and J. Timmerman. 2011. *Neogene and Quaternary Fossils of North Carolina: A Field Guide*. Raleigh: North Carolina Fossil Club.
Fuller, S. L. H., F. W. Grimm, T. L. Laavy, H. J. Porter, and A. H. Shoemaker. 1980. "Status Report: Freshwater and Terrestrial Mollusks." In *Proceedings of the First*

South Carolina Endangered Species Symposium, edited by D. M. Forsythe and W. B. Ezell Jr., 55–59. Columbia: South Carolina Endangered Species Symposium.

Lee, H. G. 2009. *Marine Shells of Northeast Florida*. Jacksonville, FL: Jacksonville Shell Club.

Mikkelsen, P. M., and R. Bieler. 2008. *Seashells of Southern Florida: Living Marine Mollusks of the Florida Keys and Adjacent Regions—Bivalves*. Princeton, NJ: Princeton University Press.

MolluscaBase. n.d. Accessed November 6, 2023. www.molluscabase.org.

North Carolina Department of Environmental Quality, Division of Marine Fisheries. n.d.a. "Fisheries Statistics." Accessed October 31, 2023. www.deq.nc.gov/about /divisions/marine-fisheries/science-and-statistics/fisheries-statistics#Commercial Statistics-4270.

———. n.d.b. "Shellfish Sanitation and Recreational Water Quality." Accessed October 31, 2023. www.deq.nc.gov/about/divisions/marine-fisheries/shellfish -sanitation-and-recreational-water-quality.

Petuch, E. J., R. F. Myers, and D. P. Berschauer. 2015. *The Living and Fossil Busycon Whelks: Iconic Mollusks of Eastern North America*. Encinitas, CA: San Diego Shell Club.

Porter, H. J. 1972. "Shell Collecting from Stomachs of the Sea-Star Genus *Astropecten*." *New York Shell Club Notes* 180: 2–4.

———. 1974. *The North Carolina Marine and Estuarine Mollusca: An Atlas of Occurrence*. Morehead City: University of North Carolina Institute of Marine Sciences.

———. 1985a. "Rare and Endangered Fauna of Lake Waccamaw, North Carolina Watershed System." In *North Carolina Endangered Species Restoration Technical Report*. Vol. 1. Raleigh: North Carolina Wildlife Resources Commission.

———. 1985b. "Rare and Endangered Fauna of Lake Waccamaw, North Carolina Watershed System: Molluscan Census and Ecological Interrelationships." In *North Carolina Endangered Species Restoration Technical Report*. Raleigh: North Carolina Wildlife Resources Commission.

———. 1989. "Continental Shelf Molluscan Zoogeography of North and South Carolina." In *North Carolina Coastal Oceanography Symposium, NOAA National Undersea Research Program, Research Report 89–2, Dec. 1989*, edited by R. Y. George and A. W. Hulbert, 231–78. Rockville, MD: National Oceanic and Atmospheric Administration.

———. 2008. "Range Extension—Zebra Periwinkle in North Carolina [Family · Littorinidae]." *Journal of the North Carolina Academy of Science* 1241:26. See current scientific classification in the species description section of this book.

Porter, H. J., and L. Houser. 1997. *Seashells of North Carolina*. Raleigh: North Carolina Sea Grant, North Carolina State University. UNC-SG-97–03.

Porter, H. J., C. Johnson, and A. B. McCrary. 1977. "Marine Invertebrates." In *Endangered and Threatened Plants and Animals of North Carolina*, edited by

J. E. Cooper, J. S. Robinson and J. S. Funderburg., 233–49. Raleigh: North Carolina Museum of Natural History.

Porter, H. J., and J. Tyler. 1971. *Seashells Common to North Carolina*. Raleigh: North Carolina Department of Natural and Economic Resources, Division of Commercial and Sports Fisheries. Reprinted 1981. UNC Sea Grant Publication UNC-SG-72-09.

Rehder, H. A. 1981. *Audubon Society Field Guide to North American Seashells*. New York: Alfred A. Knopf.

Rosenberg, G. 2014. "A New Critical Estimate of Named Species-Level Diversity of the Recent Mollusca." *American Malacological Bulletin* 32 (2): 308–22.

Solem, G. A. 1974. *The Shell Makers: Introducing Mollusks*. New York: John Wiley and Sons.

Sturm, C. F., T. A. Pearce, and A. Valdés, eds. 2006. *The Mollusks: A Guide to Their Study, Collection, and Preservation*. Irvine, CA: American Malacological Bulletin, Universal.

Tabb, K. 2018. "Our Coast's History: NC's Oyster War." *Coastal Review*, August 29, 2018. https://coastalreview.org/2018/08/our-coasts-history-ncs-oyster-war.

Timmerman, J., and R. E. Chandler. 2008. *Cretaceous and Paleogene Fossils of North Carolina: A Field Guide*. Raleigh: North Carolina Fossil Club.

———. 2020. *Fossil Mollusks*. Vol. 2. 2nd ed. Raleigh: North Carolina Fossil Club.

Turgeon, D. D., J. F. Quinn, A. E. Bogan, E. V. Coan, F. G. Hochberg, W. G. Lyons, P. M. Mikkelsen, R. J. Neves, C. F. E. Roper, G. Rosenberg, B. Roth, A. H. Scheltema, F. G. Thompson, M. Vecchione, and J. D. Williams. 1998. *Common and Scientific Names of Aquatic Invertebrates from the United States and Canada: Mollusks*. 2nd ed. Bethesda, MD: American Fisheries Society.

Wells, H. W., M. J. Wells, and I. E. Gray. 1961. "Food of the Sea-Star *Astropecten articulatus*." *Biological Bulletin* 1202:265–71.

Witherington, B., and D. Witherington. 2011. *Seashells of Georgia and the Carolinas*. Sarasota, FL: Pineapple.

Wolfe, D. A. 2014. "Hugh J. Porter: Contributions to Malacology and the North Carolina Shell Club." *American Conchologist* 42 (4): 32–35.

Yonge, C. M., and T. E. Thompson. 1926. *Living Marine Mollusca*. New York: HarperCollins.

RECOMMENDED RESOURCES

The following websites are regularly updated.

Conchologists of America. conchologistsofamerica.org.

MolluscaBase. molluscabase.org.

North Carolina Department of Environmental Quality. deq.nc.gov. Follow division links for Marine Fisheries (and page link for Fisheries Statistics) and Shellfish Sanitation and Recreational Water Quality.

North Carolina Museum of Natural Sciences. naturalsciences.org.

North Carolina Oyster Blueprint. ncoysters.org.

North Carolina Sea Grant. ncseagrant.org.

North Carolina Shell Club. ncshellclub.com. This site provides an extensive list of websites that may be helpful in identification of mollusks, local and worldwide.

Index of Common and Scientific Names

Bonnet, Coronado, 17, 150
  Scotch, xii, 9–10, 27, 148–49, 150,
    plate 25
Boonea impressa, 200
  seminuda, 200
Bostrycapulus aculeatus, 137
Botula fusca, 35
Brachidontes exustus, 35
brasiliana, Anadara, 41
brasiliense, Entodesma, 115
Bubble, 29, 197
  Common Atlantic, 198
  Striate, 198
Buccinidae, 117, 174
bufo, Bufonaria, 147
  Marsupina, 147
Bufonaria bufo, 147
bugensis, Dreissena, 15
Bulla occidentalis, 198
  striata, 198
Bullidae, 29, 117, 197
Bursidae, 28, 117, 147
Busycon carica, 160–61, plate 30
  carica eliceans, 161
  sinistrum, 164
Busyconidae, 28, 117, 160
Busycotypus canaliculatus, 161, plate 31
  spiratus, 162

Calliostoma euglyptum, 119
  pulchrum, 119
  yucatecanum, 120
Calliostomatidae, 26, 117, 118
Callucina keenae, 63
Calyptraeidae, 26, 117, 137
campechiensis, Mercenaria, 102
  Pholas, 109
canaliculata, Acteocina, 198
canaliculatus, Busycotypus, 161, plate 31
Cancellaria reticulata, 159
Cancellariidae, 28, 117, 158
cancellata, Chione, 97
candei, Acteocina, 199
candida, Barbatia, 43
canrena, Natica, 131
  Naticarius, 131

Cantharus, 28, 174
  Ribbed, 175, 177–78, plate 34
  Tinted, 174, 181
Cantharus multangulus, 175
Cardiidae, 22, 24, 31, 68
Carditid, Flattened, 66
  Threetooth, 65, 66
Carditidae, 22, 31, 65
caribaea, Coralliophila, 177
carica, Busycon, 160–61, plate 30
carica eliceans, Busycon, 161
carnea, Pinna, 50
caroliniana, Polymesoda, 76
carolinensis, Polyschides, 210
Caryocorbula contracta, 106
  nasuta, 105
  swiftiana, 105
Cassidae, 27, 117, 148, 214
Cassis madagascariensis, 148, 149,
    plate 22
  madagascariensis spinella, 149,
    plate 23
castanea, Turbo, 121
caudata, Eupleura, 178
  Linatella, 152
cayenensis, Diodora, 118
cellulosa, Favartia, 179
Cephalopoda, 5, 12, 203–4
cerinella, Cryoturris, 192
Cerith, 27, 121, 134
  Adam's Miniature, 134
  Dark, 122
  Florida, 122
  Grass, 121
Cerithiidae, 27, 117, 121
Cerithiopsidae, 27, 117, 134
Cerithium atratum, 122
Cerodrillia simpsoni, 191
cervus, Cypraea, 141
  Macrocypraea, 141, plate 18
Chaetopleura apiculata, 206
Chaetopleuridae, 203, 206
Chama congregata, 73
  macerophylla, 74
Chamidae, 23, 31, 73
championi, Epitonium, 125

delessertii, 189
ermineus, 188
floridanus f. floridensis, 188
largillierti, 187, plate 39
stearnsii, 189
convexa, Crepidula, 137
Coquina, 22, 89
  Florida, 90
  Fossor, 89
  Variable, 89–90, plate 11
Coralliophila caribaea, 177
  scalariformis, 177
Coralsnail, 27, 176
  Caribbean, 175, 177–78
  Staircase, 177
Corbicula fluminea, 15, 76
Corbula, 22–23, 105
  Contracted, 106
  Dietz, 107
  Rose, 106–7
Corbula contracta, 106
  dietziana, 106
  operculata, 106
Corbulidae, 22–23, 31, 105–6
cornuta, Arcinella, 73
coronadoi, Echinophoria, 150
corrugatum krebsii, Cymatium, 153
corrugatus, Monoplex, 153
costata, Cyrtopleura, 108
Costellariidae, 28, 117, 182
Costoanachis avara, 166
  floridana, 166
Cotonopsis lafresnayi, 167
Cowrie, 27, 140
  Atlantic Deer, 141–42, plate 18
  Atlantic Yellow, 141
Cowrie-Helmet, Reticulate, 149, plate 24
Crassatella, 22, 66
  Beautiful, 67
Crassatellidae, 22, 31, 66
Crassinella, Lunate, 67
Crassinella lunulata, 67
Crassostrea virginica, 51
crenella, Parvilucina, 65
Crepidula aculeata, 137
  convexa, 137

fornicata, 138
  maculosa, 139
  plana, 139
cristata, Tellidora, 88
cristella, Pseudochama, 74–75
Crucibulum striatum, 140
Cryoturris cerinella, 192
  fargoi, 193
Cryptostrea permollis, 53
Ctenoides mitis, 61
  scaber, 61
Cumingia, Common, 92
cumingianus, Solecurtus, 94
Cumingia sinuosa, 91–92
  tellinoides, 92
cuneata, Rangia, 78, 86
cuneiformis, Martesia, 109
Cup-and-Saucer, 26, 137
  Striate, 140
Cyclinella, Atlantic, 99
  Thin, 99
Cyclinella tenuis, 99
cydia, Drillia, 192
  Neodrillia, 192
Cymatiidae, 28, 117, 151–52
Cymatium cingulatum, 152
  corrugatum krebsii, 153
  parthenopeum, 154
Cyphoma, 27, 142
  McGinty's, 142
Cyphoma gibbosum, 143
  mcgintyi, 142
Cypraecassis testiculus, 149, plate 24
Cypraea cervus, 141
  spurca acicularis, 142
Cypraeidae, 27, 117, 140, 142
Cyrenoididae, 22, 31, 76
Cyrtopleura costata, 108

Dallocardia muricata, 69
Datemussel, Giant, 38
  Mahogany, 37
  Scissor, 35, 37–38
delessertii, Conasprella, 188, plate 40
  Conus, 189
demissa, Geukensia, 36

Other **Southern Gateways Guides** you might enjoy

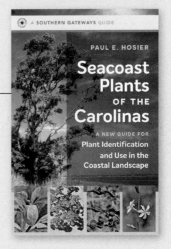

Seacoast Plants of the Carolinas

A New Guide for Plant Identification and
Use in the Coastal Landscape

PAUL E. HOSIER

Published in association with North Carolina Sea Grant

The must-have guide for plant lovers along the North Carolina coast

Thirty Great North Carolina Science Adventures

From Underground Wonderlands to Islands
in the Sky and Everything in Between

Edited by **APRIL C. SMITH**

SARAH J. CARRIER, *Assistant Editor*

Make your own top-ten list of adventures—and go!

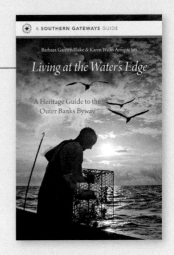

Living at the Water's Edge

A Heritage Guide to the Outer Banks Byway

**BARBARA GARRITY-BLAKE
AND KAREN WILLIS AMSPACHER**

A unique guide to the byway's people and places